HISTORY TEACHING

The Era Approach

HISTORY TEACHING

The Era Approach

BY

P. CARPENTER

M.A., B.LITT.

Assistant Tutor, Cambridge Institute of Education

CAMBRIDGE
AT THE UNIVERSITY PRESS
1964

PUBLISHED BY

THE SYNDICS OF THE CAMBRIDGE UNIVERSITY PRESS

Bentley House, 200 Euston Road, London, N.W.1
American Branch: 32 East 57th Street, New York 22, N.Y.
West African Office: P.O. Box 33, Ibadan, Nigeria

©

CAMBRIDGE UNIVERSITY PRESS

1964

Printed in Great Britain by Spottiswoode, Ballantyne & Co. Ltd.
London and Colchester

Contents

Preface

The era approach to the teaching of history may be summed up as the intensive study, on the part of the pupils, of short and unrelated passages of time. In the schools into which it has found its way, primary as well as secondary, it is known by various names or, more often than not, by no particular name. This is significant, for attempts to attach a label to it have not been altogether successful. Of the labels most frequently used, two (project and period) are too vague, and the others (topic and patch) too restricted in concept.

The word 'project' (sometimes known as 'centre of interest') conjures up in the minds of many teachers an undertaking of group activity on a grand scale, in which more than one subject in the school curriculum is involved. The term 'period' is also misleading, since it is by definition a portion of the time the length of which is indefinite, unless specifically stated. It is then usually associated with the historical periods offered for examination purposes.

'Topic' does not meet the case either, for it is commonly understood to refer to a specific theme which, for the purpose of closer inspection, has been taken out of its chronological or contemporary context. Nor is a more recent label, 'patch', entirely satisfactory. In the first place, it is inelegant, suggesting something scrappy. Furthermore, though originally intended to denote the treatment in depth of particular ages, it is often identified with units of work *within* these ages.

Much confusion has resulted from the indiscriminate use of the above terms, and it is to avoid adding to the confusion that the neutral term 'era' has been chosen. Apart from this initial act of baptism, no originality can be claimed. The practices which are discussed are already well established in the classroom, and the issues that lie behind them have occupied the minds of countless generations of history teachers.

The purpose of the present book is not to advocate the era approach as the solution to the problems of teaching history in schools, but to give a factual description of it and to attempt to make an objective assessment. In order to arrive at this assessment, it has been necessary to go into the question of selection of historical material as a whole and to refer at some length to more traditional ways of presenting the subject. The temptation to make a comparison with other departures from tradition has, however, been resisted. For to do them justice would have entailed subjecting them to an equally searching examination, and that was clearly outside the compass of this book.

Finally, a word on how the book came to be written. As a schoolmaster, the author became increasingly dissatisfied with the type of history teaching he inherited and experimented with a number of alternatives. Later on, at the Oxford University Department of Education, he was fortunate to be a colleague of Miss R. M. Goodrich who did some interesting work with her students along era lines. What eventually decided him to put pen to paper was his inability to suggest a book on the approach when asked to do so in the course of his lecturing.

If what follows should go some way towards filling a gap, it is thanks not only to Miss Goodrich, but to the extraordinarily generous help received from Mr T. Cairns, of Sunderland Training College, which can never be adequately acknowledged. The author is also indebted to Mr G. L. Middleton, of the Cambridge Institute of Education, for his assistance with proof reading.

P. C.

May, 1964

1

The Foundations of the
History Syllabus

Many arguments have been advanced to justify the inclusion of history in the school curriculum, but ultimately all of them stem from the claim that the study of the past contributes to a better understanding of the present. This claim can be substantiated on purely practical as well as general cultural grounds.

There is, first of all, the utilitarian motive which springs from the recognition that the structure of our present-day society and the issues that confront it have their origins in the past. The better our knowledge of these origins is, the better equipped we are, it is argued, to discharge the responsibilities to which we are committed as members of that society.

At the same time, the above claim applies equally to those people who wish for no more than that delving into the past should satisfy their curiosity and give them pleasure. Even if they cannot be shown to derive any immediate and tangible benefits from doing so, the imaginative experience involved cannot but enrich their minds. It may be said that one who has passed through such an experience and in the course of it acquired a general background knowledge, is better placed to understand the times in which he lives than one who has not.

History, let it be remembered, is concerned with the present as much as with the past, and any dichotomy between them is false since there is a continuous process of the one merging into the other. Hence, there is general agreement that this process presents a worthwhile and indeed

1

necessary subject for study and that it should form an integral part of everyone's education.

But as soon as it is realized what this study entails difficulties set in. For if history is the story of the development of the present-day world, it is the story of human endeavour, of political institutions, international relations, social conditions, scientific progress, etc. History is all that, and much more. What chance is there of doing justice to such a range, even if it were possible to devote a whole lifetime to it?

It is at this point that we come face to face with the problem of selection. We cannot regard all facts relating to the past as being of equal importance, but must select those which are of more significance than others. Here the word 'significance' is used in a subjective sense, as it applies to us living in the second half of the twentieth century.

We use our judgment in the light of such knowledge as we possess, and we interpret our knowledge in the light of current attitudes and concepts, which means that we must be prepared to see the next generation of students of history arriving at different conclusions. The transient nature of what is historically significant can be illustrated by the following example.

At a time when one after the other of Britain's former colonies is reaching the goal of independence, there is of necessity much preoccupation with the reorientation of the British Empire and Commonwealth and hence a renewed interest in its evolution. It is not unreasonable to suppose that when the old ties with the mother country have been severed, the present interest will lessen and that Imperialism, much maligned today, will be regarded in retrospect as a necessary and even beneficial stage on the road to national maturity. By then the focus of attention will be on other problems relating to the contemporary world, with a corresponding adjustment as to what aspects of the past receive closer consideration.

Having experienced so many changes in our own lifetime, we can never be sure that by the time the children of today have become the adults of tomorrow, the issues will still be as topical and relevant as they are at this moment. What we may be sure of is that at every stage the quest for historical information will be affected, however imperceptibly, by the preoccupations of the time in question.

So far history has been mentioned only in terms of studying it, as distinct from teaching it. The teaching aspect introduces further complications, in that those in charge of the subject have to exercise their judgment not for themselves but on behalf of others; these are not adults like themselves, but children; and the time at their disposal is extremely limited. In quantitive terms alone, what boys and girls come into contact with while they are at school can only be a part, a very minute part, of the story of man. The task of selection is thus made harder, and it becomes evident that factors other than historical values are at stake.

Indeed, the question of what material should go into the syllabus and the grounds on which it is selected cannot be answered in terms of the subject alone. Consideration must be given to a number of criteria, and it is the purpose of the following pages to discuss what these are.

At the outset, one general observation may not be amiss: care should be taken at all times to ensure factual accuracy and to treat with caution any of the romanticized stories which are sometimes passed off as history. This is not to belittle the value of good historical fiction which has done much to stimulate an interest in the subject. Fiction fulfils a supplementary function and can do this admirably. The point is that, no matter how good a story may be, if it does not record what actually happened, it does not belong to the category of history.

The first, and by far the most important factor against which to measure the matter to be selected, is the pupils we teach, their capacity and interest. It is always tempting to talk of 'the child' as if he were a specimen capable of being scientifically examined and labelled. No such child exists, and what a teacher has to remember throughout is that he is dealing with individual children.

It is also easy to exaggerate differences in interest as related to age and mental ability. What little evidence there is goes to show that these interests differ in degree rather than in kind. That is to say, at all stages children find it hard to muster an enthusiasm for constitutional (as distinct from political) issues, whilst the human and romantic elements retain their fascination throughout life, as is witnessed by the popularity of biographies and stories of war, travel and adventure. Nor are the responses of girls so markedly different from those of boys as one might be inclined to think. The observations which follow are, therefore, of a very general nature only.

From their infancy children show an absorbing interest in other people, and to identify themselves with them forms an essential part in the development of their character. Because of this human concern, the lessons will be focused initially on the lives and deeds of famous figures of the past. This ensures a ready response and provides a useful lead into an understanding of the age to which they made a contribution.

Whenever possible, these figures should be actual historical characters or, alternatively, representatives of their class or profession, as found in the *Canterbury Tales*. 'The People' is a generalization which amounts to an abstraction and carries little appeal. Also, and this need present no serious obstacle whilst the subject is not yet treated methodically, examples should be chosen from countries all over the world, lest the impression be gained that human achievement is the prerogative of any particular nation.

One major difficulty which bedevils the teacher at every turn is that all the characters on the historical stage belong

4

to the world of adults. It is true that the nature of ambition, fear or loyalty can be appreciated from an early age, but the springs which motivate human action usually go deeper than that, and to grasp all the subtleties involved requires a more mature mind.

Is the answer, then, to subordinate events to conditions? Not altogether, for what fascinates a child is not so much how people live as what they do, even if he does not understand why they do it. There was a time when there was an over-emphasis on the latter, which gave rise to that masterpiece of historical satire *1066 And All That*, but it may be that the pendulum has swung too far in the opposite (that is 'social') direction.

Boys and girls have an almost unlimited capacity for exercising their imagination, which is easily fired by things however strange or remote. In fact, their lack of preconception often enables them to feel more at home in the past—prehistorical times in particular—than their more sophisticated elders. By stimulating the imaginative faculty, the range of their experience can be extended. Whenever possible, the attempt should be made to link imaginative experiences with experiences of everyday life and to follow up any clue which the local and social environment may offer for exploring the past. The importance of using the familiar as the point of departure cannot be overstressed. But to concentrate on it to the exclusion of everything else would be a mistake.

In the first place, the natural curiosity which children possess is far too great to confine itself to matters which are familiar to them. On the contrary, it is the unusual which often has the greater attraction. Besides, the range of their actual experience is still very limited, and the environment in which many of them are brought up offers little scope for enlarging it. It does not by any means follow that, just because something is close at hand, whether in space or in time, it thereby carries a greater appeal or is more easily understood.

Irrespective of whether the information comes from near or far, there is more likelihood of its being meaningful to youngsters if they are allowed to handle it in some way; and once it has acquired meaning, the foundations are laid for the process of finding out for themselves. Although, at first, the story as told by the teacher or read in a book will quite properly occupy a prominent place, it is from an early age that children learn by expressing themselves. What is included in the syllabus should, therefore, also be chosen with an eye to any opportunities that may present themselves for inviting their active participation, be it through drawing, building or play-acting. For these, some material is obviously more suited than other. The course of the Hundred Years' War, for instance, can be expressed more easily in concrete or visible terms than the causes.

In general, the demands made on young pupils must not be too exacting, for their span of concentration is short and ability to perceive relationships not yet fully developed. It is best to regard the early years as a period of initiation with the object of kindling an interest, and not to attempt to teach the subject formally and in a systematic way.

It has already been remarked that, as we follow children through their development, no sudden transformations can be observed. But as they grow older their interest in, and comprehension of, the significance of cause and effect grow too, so that it becomes possible to take them behind the scenes, as it were, and show them not only what happened but why it happened. And whereas the emphasis has hitherto been on material things and the approach largely biographical or even anecdotal, there is a whole world of ideas beyond to which their minds can gradually be opened.

Now, too, is the time for more attention to the particular, when children not only ask all sorts of penetrating questions —which they have done from the beginning—but are not satisfied until the required details are supplied. The material must be such, therefore, that it can be explored in depth. It must be more advanced in other respects as well, because their heightened capacity for reasoned thought and mastery of expression enables them to rely more on their own efforts. At the same time, their abilities tend to run in more individual channels, which underlines the need for variety, so that each one of them may be stimulated to express his full potential.

Yet, whereas their faculty for projecting themselves into the world of yesterday remains undiminished, boys and girls are often less willing to exercise this faculty as they grow older. This is because, with their future careers ahead of them, the world around them begins to loom more largely in their minds, and what affects them directly has the greater impact. Whilst it does not mean that what went on before should be neglected in favour of what is happening at the moment, every effort must be made to establish the bonds which inextricably link the present with the past. The bonds are often anything but apparent, which makes the task all the harder.

It takes a long time before that degree of maturity is reached when young people can weigh up evidence for them-selves and use their judgment independently and critically, and when the issues underlying historical situations begin to fall into place. Such things can be expected in the sixth form, aided by a more generous allowance in the time-table and smaller numbers in the class. Then, too, through mak-ing a comparative study of different writers handling the same raw material, they may learn something of the historian's craft. As for the power he wields, they may even agree with Samuel Butler that 'although God cannot alter the past, historians can; it is perhaps because they can be useful to Him in this respect that He tolerates their existence'![1]

But in this connection a note of warning must be struck. It is as easy—and as mistaken—to keep adolescents on apron strings for too long, as it is to assume that they are

[1] *Erewhon Revisited*, Ch. 14.

as much at home with abstractions as they were, in their younger days, with concrete material.

Apart from the pupils' age—mental rather than chronological—their level of intelligence must be taken into account. With less bright children, and this applies to all age-levels, it is imperative that a number of modifications are introduced into the scheme of work. The first, and most obvious, is to be wary of intricate questions such as are posed by constitutional or religious matters. This is because their comparative lack of imagination, reasoning power and ability to grasp relationships makes it harder for them to visualize something that cannot be directly observed.

Secondly, it is necessary to proceed at a slower working pace, the effect of which is that, unless the number of teaching periods is substantially increased, the amount of subject matter tackled is much less. It would be a waste of time, because psychologically unsound, to attempt to cover the same ground by treating it less thoroughly. It is all the more important that, as with young children, there should be scope for as detailed and concrete a treatment as possible.

Many issues have to be simplified, but there are limits to which one can go and it is often better to leave alone what cannot be readily explained. In fact, the axe of selection must be wielded in an even more ruthless manner with these children than with their more gifted fellows. A 'C' stream course which is a watered-down version of the 'A' stream course will never do.

Finally, it must not be forgotten that history has an emotional as well as intellectual content, and just as we cannot afford to ignore differences in ability, we cannot ignore the attitudes that are formed towards it. An initially positive attitude is quickly changed into a negative one if the material is inappropriate or, indeed, if suitable material is presented in an unimaginative way. Fortunately, the past provides such varied fare that even the most extravagant taste is capable of being satisfied. If this does not happen, it is not the fault of the subject.

This is not to say that the steps we take should be dictated by the children's whims, or their likes and dislikes. These are transitory and subject to environmental changes. It is, in truth, a weakness of the so-called child-centred approach in education that it is apt to take spontaneous reactions at their face value and is not sufficiently outward- and forward-looking.

From a discussion of children, we now turn to the person of the teacher, for it is he who, whatever pressures are brought to bear on him, is finally responsible for drawing up and administering the syllabus. The better his qualifications, the better are his prospects of successfully discharging his responsibilities, the term 'qualifications' here being used in the sense of being a blend of training, knowledge, enthusiasm and ability.

Thorough familiarity with the basic facts must be the ultimate object, and for that reason the trained specialist has, as in every other profession, a considerable advantage. The non-specialist, on the other hand, may be more sensitive to what is required—he does not fall so readily into the trap of taking for granted that what his pupils ought to know, and what he himself knows, are the same thing.

Any deficiency in factual knowledge can be made up in time. More important is a willingness to add to the knowledge and ability to utilize it. Everything that has been learnt at the training college or university, a young teacher finds, has to be re-appraised, and it takes many years of experience in the classroom before he can begin to feel confident that he is operating at a level which does justice to both the subject and the pupils.

Apart from qualifying in the above-mentioned sense, a teacher is always at his best at those things which fill him with a genuine enthusiasm. Such enthusiasm is infectious, and whether it be for medieval castles or modern railways, there is every prospect that, provided it is not a fad, it will transmit itself to his charges. What may at first seem like a by-way, may in fact be the gateway into the past. A teacher with a special interest in archaeology will no doubt make as much as he can of the opportunities the local environment may offer. For another, digging for prehistoric remains may have no appeal whatever, and it would be foolish of him to attempt any serious work in that direction.

Important, also, are differences in ability. One who possesses the gift of narration will choose his material with an eye to the impact he knows a well-told story makes on his young listeners. For another, dramatic representation may be the most natural and effective medium. An enthusiasm, however passionately felt, is of little avail unless it is matched by the ability to put it to good purpose. These two, enthusiasm and ability, do not necessarily go together, but when they do, they make an irresistible combination.

The discussion would not be complete without reference to certain external factors which have a bearing on the amount and nature of the material to be selected. For instance, the number of periods available in the time-table will impose limits on how much it is possible to achieve. Over the years, it makes quite a difference whether the allowance is two periods a week or three, and in a school which enjoys the more generous allocation it is reasonable to expect that more ground is covered.

Not only does this depend on the number of lessons per week, but on the length of the course at the post-primary stage. This may be anything from four years in some secondary modern schools to eight years in some grammar schools. Occasionally, history is not taken as a compulsory subject throughout, but is dropped during the last year or two. Again, allowance has to be made for the fact that there are two leaving dates for the fifteen-year olds (at Easter and in

July), when planning the syllabus for the fourth year of a four-year course.

In this context, consideration must be given to the requirements of external examinations, where these are taken. Although it may appear so at first sight, it does by no means follow that a teacher loses control over the syllabus as soon as he enters his pupils for an examination which he has not set himself.

In the first place, there is no compulsion to do so, but if it is decided to take the step, there are a number of national examining boards to choose from. All of them offer alternative papers in history, so that the teacher is at liberty to select from the board of his choice the paper which he regards as the most appropriate. Each board has its own machinery to make sure that when a syllabus is first drafted, or subsequently revised, this is not done without consulting the teaching profession. What is more, if a school does not like any of the existing papers, it is entitled to submit for approval an alternative syllabus more closely in accordance with its own curriculum.

It is true that once a syllabus has been subscribed to, it must be strictly adhered to, but that does not warrant the complaint which is sometimes made about the 'cramping' effect of examination requirements.[1] In any case, these affect pupils only towards the end of their career, since the actual preparation for the event does not take longer than a year, or two years at the most.

There need not be any such fears where an examination is taken which is organized on a local or regional basis. There are various kinds of these. In many of them the papers are set and scripts marked by the teachers themselves, and the marks moderated by an outside panel of assessors in order to ensure that the standards are comparable.

The above remarks do not, of course, apply to the primary school, but in preparatory schools, in which pupils are pre-

---

[1] But see also page 27.

pared for the 'Common Examination for Entrance to Public Schools', the position is different. The history paper which forms part of that examination never varies. The questions cover the whole range of British history from 55 B.C. to the present day, with the result that syllabuses in use in preparatory schools are more stereotyped.

Another factor which should have a bearing on the question of selection is the locality and the opportunity it offers. It will not be surprising if Anglo-Scottish relations do not loom so largely in schools in Kent or Cornwall, as they do north of the River Tyne. And if elsewhere special attention is paid to recent economic trends, it may be more than a coincidence that this is in Lancashire.

Each area has historical associations of its own, and the traditions of a school can be reflected by its local background in many subtle ways. When taking up a new appointment, there are many good reasons why a teacher should wish to go to a particular place; its locality may be amongst the more important considerations if he is keen on local history.

Finally, though this should never be the overriding factor, the planning of the course may be helped, or hindered, by the availability or otherwise of certain aids to teaching. Some approaches depend on a plentiful supply of reference books devoted to specific topics, while others lean heavily on the use of pictorial and other illustrative material.

The fruits which a systematic study of the past may be expected to yield; the intrinsic character of history as a subject in its own right; the varied abilities and interests of the children who are undertaking the study; the teachers whose task it is to guide them through that study; examinations as an attempt to supply a standard of assessment; the schools which provide the setting—all these are factors to which careful consideration must be given when the policy of syllabus construction is being framed, and all of them involve different criteria for selection.

To consider each criterion separately is one thing; to weigh up their respective claims, which has to be done when it comes to applying the criteria, is another matter altogether. As soon as that step is taken, it becomes obvious that many of them conflict with one another. It is small wonder that there are differences of opinion not only regarding what material is to be selected *for* the syllabus, but how the material is to be arranged *within* the syllabus, not to speak of the manner in which it is to be presented. These differences exist, but when the actual syllabuses in use in schools are examined, a greater degree of uniformity is found than might have been supposed.

2

The Traditional Syllabus and its Origin

In most schools the view prevails that, since the present has developed out of the past, the study of history should be a study in development. Hence the attempt is made to trace the story of mankind, with particular reference to the national scene, from the earliest times to the present day in a continuous sequence.

Within the chronological framework the treatment varies not only, as could hardly be otherwise, between primary and secondary schools or between different kinds of secondary schools, but also between one modern school and another and one grammar school and another. For that reason it is impossible to be specific. But the following summary, which is based on an inquiry conducted by UNESCO,[1] gives a reliable, if generalized picture of the kind of history with which a child may be expected to come into contact during the years of compulsory attendance in this country.

In the primary school, the introduction into the realm of history is usually made from the age of seven upwards, through the lives and deeds of outstanding people of the past, chosen from any age or country. It is also customary to introduce Juniors to their present local and social environment, by relating it to an inquiry into the conditions under which their forefathers used to dwell, dress or travel. Gradually, more and more material is incorporated and a time sequence established, so that when a child leaves the

---

[1] *History, Geography and Social Studies.* A summary of school programmes in fifty-three countries. UNESCO, 1953.

primary school at the age of eleven he will have completed the journey through the past for the first time.

If, on the other hand, he attends a preparatory school, he will remain there for another two to three years, during which the ground previously covered is generally traversed at a more advanced level.

It is not till the secondary stage is reached that history can be said to be treated in any systematic way. Here children find themselves in different types of schools, and which course they follow depends also on such factors as how long they stay on and whether they are expected to take an external examination before they leave. Generally speaking, the material is presented chronologically and is built round a spinal core of British history, to which as much World history is added as time permits.

The chronological survey is divided into a number of periods. In number, the periods vary according to the length of the course, and in extent, according to the degree of importance attached to them. If the course comprises five years, the work may be distributed as follows:

> Year 1: Pre-history to the fall of Rome
> Year 2: The Middle Ages
> Year 3: Tudors and Stuarts
> Year 4: The 18th and early 19th Centuries
> Year 5: The 19th and 20th Centuries

If the course is of four years' duration, the periods are correspondingly adjusted, for example: pre-history–1066; 1066–1714; 1714–1870; 1870–1945. Other syllabuses follow different time divisions, but these do not affect the principle of a continuous course progressing through the centuries.

Sometimes the chronological survey is completed in three or even two years, the remainder being devoted to the study of one or more of the following: the contemporary world; recent developments from a social or economic point of view; local history; central and local government; or selected topics such as exploration or housing through the ages.

Further examples of deviations from the chronological British-cum-World history arrangement could be cited, but despite some loss in popularity, the latter continues to enjoy a firm hold over the syllabuses of schools all over the British Isles. This remarkable predominance can be explained if we take a look at the growth of history as a subject in the school curriculum.

Since at least Tudor times, the study of the past had been used as an instrument for instructing children in moral values and patriotic virtues. But being traditionally regarded as a branch of literature, history was not taught in its own right until well into the middle of the nineteenth century. Even then it is true to say that the Victorians were better at making history than at teaching it! When it finally made its appearance in the time-table (largely as a result of its being recognized as a degree subject at Oxford and Cambridge), the accent remained on national events, with the object of showing the emergence of Britain as a great power as well as the guardian of liberty.

The emphasis was, consequently, on military and diplomatic affairs to make the first point, and on constitutional and political affairs to make the second. In terms of content, this meant that what was offered consisted largely of chronicles of wars and battles, treaties and alliances, successive ministries and acts of parliaments, and reigns of kings and queens. The attitude to the subject may have been a narrow one, but there was at least this to be said in its favour: the subject matter was clearly defined and of manageable proportions, and the teacher did not have to worry about his ability to cope in the time available to him.

With the approach of the twentieth century, however, there emerged a new concept of the scope and function of history. This was to have far-reaching effects, in that the body of knowledge which had hitherto passed for history grew beyond recognition, the growth being extended simultaneously in a number of directions.

In the first place, there was an extension in breadth because the view, made famous by Carlyle's dictum, 'No great man lives in vain. The History of the world is but the Biography of great men',[1] went out of fashion and it was no longer thought that the events of the past could be explained simply by reference to the decisions and actions of a few individuals. According to a new, determinist school of thought, these were not seen as shaping their nation's destiny but acting as a mouthpiece for the aspirations of their times.

The interest shifted to the ordinary people: their lives and struggles and their collective impact on the course of events. Even they were seen as, essentially, the product of their conditions which, in turn, were shaped by what it became fashionable to call 'underlying trends', for example economic pressures, social factors, scientific and technical progress and cultural developments. The recognition of the significance of these trends challenged the traditional syllabus, which had for so long been monopolized by political and military matters and the kings, ministers or generals who conducted them.

The latter were forced to give way, but were by no means ousted. That this is so is shown by the fact that most key dates still have political associations, and whereas a figure such as Napoleon is part of history as the term is commonly understood, Sir Isaac Newton and Leonardo da Vinci are regarded as belonging to the special provinces of the history of Science and Art respectively.

Secondly, the syllabus was extended from a geographical standpoint. Hitherto there had appeared to be no need to

---

[1] *Lectures on Heroes.* I: The Hero as Divinity.

refer to other countries at all, unless they and Britain were engaged in warlike operations. An example is China which was practically unheard of for centuries until, in the nineteenth, it was accorded three brief mentions. Or developments outside the British Isles were only described at length if these developments were of such a nature that they affected the course of events at home, and a knowledge of them was necessary for the national history to make sense.

However, under the impact of two world wars, the advent of the U.S.A. and U.S.S.R. as world powers, the awakening of nationalism in Asia and Africa and the shrinkage of the world due to advances in communications, the affairs of one nation became more and more the affairs of all the nations. The insular view of Britain as the centre of civilization was no longer tenable, and the necessity of considering other countries and other continents in their own right became increasingly clear. But there was no question of the mother country relinquishing her prior claim.

It became the object not only to impart the story of our national heritage, but to show the place of that heritage in the heritage common to all mankind and to prepare for living in a world community. The result was that at the same time as familiar ground was being surveyed from new points of view, additional room had to be found for entirely new matter which appeared on the home market and threatened to swamp it.

The third extension was in depth, when the view gained ground that, as J. B. Bury expressed it, 'history is a science, no less and no more'.[1] Professional historians became more conscious of the need for care when examining their evidence and set about their work in a more detached and methodical fashion than had been customary. If a case was to be presented or theory demolished, a firm factual foundation was

[1] Regius Professor of Modern History, University of Cambridge, in his inaugural lecture in 1903.

now regarded as a prerequisite. At the same time, previously unexplored sources of information were tapped, such as parish registers and family archives, and modern aids invoked, such as aerial photography, and even electronic computing machines for deciphering ancient hieroglyphic scripts.

As a result, a great wealth of new, and often significant, data became available, filling gaps where these had existed, confirming some facts hitherto regarded as doubtful and challenging others which had been sacrosanct for generations. (For example, recent findings of Roman settlements in the Scottish Lowlands indicate that the army of occupation was not *forced* to keep to Hadrian's Wall.) The newly-discovered data were minutely detailed and often remained uncollated and uninterpreted, for not a few historians took the view that this job was outside their terms of reference.

Others were content to catalogue alternative versions without committing themselves to any of them. This was in accord with a current wave of scepticism which expressed itself in the refusal to take on trust any premise accepted until then. The 'scientific' outlook was, therefore, applied also to known data, but many modern writers, for example the Dutch historian Huizinga, held that what their inquiries yielded were the answers to 'what' and 'how', but not to 'why', and shied away from drawing conclusions.

In a sense, this was an advance over their predecessors who had been so sure that they held the key to all the answers. But it did not make it any easier for those whose job it was to make the past intelligible to the general public, who were faced with the unenviable task of keeping up with the copious literature and found that efforts to apply rigorously the standards and methods of science often led to a deterioration in literary quality. Then they had to pick their way amongst the controversies which inevitably ensued. Attempts to rehabilitate Thomas Cromwell, for long the villain of the dissolution of the monasteries, and to debunk the cult of

Simon de Montfort as the father of representative government, are cases in point. Once it was accepted that everything that qualified as recorded fact owed its existence to
a combination of numerous and subtle influences and was
capable, moreover, of being variously interpreted, it was
no longer possible to treat in a straightforward manner what,
in the eyes of our forefathers, had been plain issues.

Finally, the span of history was extended as reckoned
by the measurement of time. Previously, a convenient starting
point for introducing children to their national heritage had
been the year in which the Romans first set foot on British
soil. Archaeologists and other research workers helped to
change all that when they produced evidence of human
life dating well back beyond the dawn of civilization and
thus opened up a new world, the existence of which had
been little more than guessed at. The fact that we refer to
these as *pre*-historical times serves as a reminder that they are
an adjunct to what is still largely regarded as 'legitimate'
history.

A corresponding development took place at the other
end of the time scale where, until recently, courses came to
an end with the death of Queen Victoria or, at the latest,
the outbreak of World War I. The practice was justified
on the grounds that distance safeguarded objectivity. If
there was some truth in this, it was also true that it left pupils
under the delusion that history stopped at some arbitrarily-
chosen date, and in ignorance of the immediate background
of the contemporary scene.

A growing body of opinion favoured extending the syllabus
to the present day, which meant that the events of each
successive year were added to the existing ones. Not surprisingly, since more was known about our own times than
those that went before and more importance was attached
to them, the additional years were treated in greater detail,
quite out of proportion to their number.

The outcome of the changes described above was that within the space of less than a hundred years, the body of historical knowledge grew to encyclopaedic dimensions, requiring an army of specialists to administer it. During that period, it is true, the school leaving age was raised twice, but the two extra years were far from sufficient to absorb all the material clamouring for admission. It was left to the teacher in the classroom to work out the practical implications of this growth, and, as we can see now, the responsibility for transmitting the knowledge to his pupils placed him in a dilemma.

The nature of this dilemma can be illustrated by reference to the Hadow Report,[1] which welcomed the broadening of the history syllabus but did not face the consequences. Due acknowledgement was made, on the one hand, to the 'difficulty. . . involved in the amount of material that it is possible to present. Time demands that this shall be extremely small in proportion to the whole.' Hence, 'large omissions' must be expected. But almost in the same breath, the schools were reminded of their duty to 'secure that no large factor should be entirely omitted. . . . The whole period, at least from the time of the Romans to the present, should be covered in some form.'

How were the teachers to resolve this conflict, for were they not encouraged to be strictly selective and, at the same time, all-embracing in their approach? The course most of them followed was to make the capacity of the existing framework the chief criterion. A number of factors were responsible for this.

To begin with, a syllabus built on the chronological plan had the virtue of being a well-ordered and safe one. There was, on the one hand, the recorded past which extended over x centuries. The time-table, on the other, allowed for y lesson periods a week for z years at school. All these were known measurements for purposes of calculation, and with

---

[1] Report of the Consultative Committee on *The Education of the Adolescent*, H.M.S.O., 1927, pp. 199, 200.

their help a structure could be erected into which the available material could be fitted systematically. A scheme which followed this precept was not only easy to draw up, but, provided the teacher knew how to organize his material, easy to adhere to.

Underlying was a deep-rooted conviction that there was such a thing as a body of essential knowledge which had to be mastered before a child's education could be regarded as complete. Accordingly, no one was to go out into the world without having been introduced to the principal characters and events of the past with their accompanying dates; and the more of these were assembled under one roof, it was thought, the greater was the likelihood of the object being achieved.

In this tradition most of those responsible for teaching the subject were brought up. Whilst they were *in statu pupillari* they experienced passing through the chronological cycle at least three times: first at the primary school, then at the secondary school, and finally at the training college or university. By that time it seemed an obvious plan to follow and, when they entered the teaching profession, it was the plan they tended to adopt themselves. Any other would have entailed abandoning much that was old and tried, and to accept responsibility for the 'large omissions' appeared a risk which not many were willing to take.

It was not only their background which predisposed teachers towards following in the footsteps of their predecessors, but their principal aid in presenting the subject, the textbook. School textbooks were descended from the standard Histories of the times, which explains why they were arranged along chronological lines. The arrangement was—and to a large extent still is—that, if together they constituted a series, each volume covered a certain period of time, beginning where the other left off.

In the days when textbooks were the chief source of instruction in class, the association between them and the conventional approach was indeed a close one. They were written with a view to facilitating orthodox teaching methods which, in turn, were designed to link up with well established and readily available reading matter. The one served to perpetuate the other.

A similar relationship existed with regard to external examinations taken by secondary schools. If the paper set by a board was an 'outlines' paper, that is the questions were spread over a wide chronological range, a knowledge of the entire range was of course demanded. If, on the other hand, the syllabus allowed for a number of limited periods into which British (and/or European) history was divided, these divisions too fitted in conveniently with the traditional arrangement of working in successive stages up to the present day. It is no coincidence that, where a choice of periods exists today, the overwhelming majority of candidates attempt questions from those dating after 1763.[1]

Apart from historical reasons which militated against making drastic changes in existing practice, there were some good educational reasons for not doing so. Was it not logical to take the events of the past in the order in which they occurred, so that the relationship which bound them in time was preserved and cause and effect followed one another in natural succession? In this way a sequence was set up in which the course of human development was shown to be continuous, since it could be traced from earliest beginnings right through to present times, as a connected whole.

The arrangement entailed that a more detailed study of modern times was deferred until the pupils had reached the upper school, for which the following advantages could be claimed: The more advanced stage a civilization reached, the more complex it became, as could be illustrated by the economic organization of a modern nation state, the prosperity of which depended on its industrial output and ability to compete in a world market. Complexities of this nature

---

[1] This has been confirmed by an inquiry conducted by the writer in 1962.

could not be grasped by immature minds, and it was therefore argued that the course should be so timed that children tackled the later periods only when they had reached a more mature stage in their mental development.

Furthermore, though sometimes a particular aspect of contemporary society could be illuminated more clearly by reference to the more remote past, it was in the eighteenth, nineteenth and twentieth centuries that most of the immediate background was to be found. These centuries should be studied, therefore, when the pupils were in the best position to understand them and relate them to the world to which they belonged.

It must not be inferred from the discussion of the teacher's dilemma arising out of the growth of the syllabus, that there was a specific time at which a choice was demanded of him. If there was a choice, it was never as clear-cut as it is today to us who in retrospect can see the transformation which took place amounting almost to a revolution. For the changes which came over the subject did not strike the schools with a sudden impact. On the contrary, they were so gradual that the consequences were not immediately apparent and many people were not aware of them. And so it was that the traditional syllabus was carried forward year after year.

Nor would it be true to say that the response of the teachers consisted merely of throwing everything that appeared on the historical market over the years into the melting pot. The sheer bulk alone forced them to be discriminating, but on the whole it is true to say that the measures they took to 'screen' the subject matter were not sufficiently methodical and, hence, not sufficiently drastic. Because it was assumed throughout that a chronological framework must at all costs be maintained, too little attention was paid to what went into the framework. What progress was made—and there was much—was in the field of method rather than matter.

Keeping the chronological framework intact and fitting into it as much material as the total capacity would allow meant that the substance had to be, as it were, dehydrated. For it was out of the question to devote the same amount of detailed attention to the entire range of world affairs as had been possible to devote to British political affairs in the days when they provided the staple diet in the syllabus. It is from this 'dehydration' that most of the objections to the conventional approach spring.

3

A Criticism of the Traditional Syllabus

To begin with, the syllabus is open to objection on the grounds that it subordinates the claims of the children to the claims of the subject.

The professional historian, it is true, owes his allegiance first and foremost to the subject of his choice and does not rest content until he is in possession of all the evidence available to him. To expect the same of children, however, is unreasonable as well as unproductive, because many of the facts do not make any sense to them. It is sometimes argued that this does not matter since, when they are older, everything will naturally fall into place.

The above argument is based on a fallacy. There will be nothing to fall into place, for it is pointless to expect retention of what, at the time of learning, was devoid of meaning. Any action based on this belief is more likely to produce a lasting dislike of history, just as the learning of nonsense syllables does not instil an appreciation of poetry. In either case, the paramount part played by interest in the process of learning is ignored, and where there is no meaning there is no interest.

In all, too much reliance is placed on the capacity of boys and girls to remember what they were once taught at school, and this applies also to many of the issues the meaning of which was grasped at the time. The amount of material 'caught' is nothing like the amount of material 'taught', which can be said of any subject in the curriculum, and history is no exception. Indeed, what we remember from our own history lessons in terms of factual knowledge is remarkably little. As fact is piled on fact in quick succession, there is not enough opportunity for applying the information (other than reproducing it occasionally for examination purposes), nor time for consolidation, revision and checking the depth of understanding. Perhaps fortunately, nature provides a corrective by allowing us to forget old data almost as fast as we learn new data.

In history it is easier than in other subjects to escape the consequences. In mathematics, for instance, the basic processes of addition and subtraction which were acquired in the early stages, are constantly re-applied, and in foreign languages certain elements of grammar must be mastered before further progress can be made. History, on the other hand, is not a structural subject and there is no such ground work to which constant reference must necessarily be made and into which new material and new concepts have to be integrated, at least at school level. For that reason it is possible to study any period picked out at random and pass an external examination on it, without any knowledge of the events that either preceded or followed it.

In view of this, one would have expected the subject to be less influenced by examinations than in fact it is. The notion that the school course should be a scaled-down version of the university course, or at least orientated towards it, still lingers on; and since doubts have been raised about the suitability of the traditional university course for those who follow it, it cannot really be defended as meeting the needs of the vast majority of children who will never specialize in history.

There are two ways in which external examinations can make their presence felt lower down in the school, with sometimes unhappy results. The first is when the entire syllabus is built round the particular period on which the pupils are going to be tested, and the other when the 'Give an account of the foreign policy of Lord Palmerston' type of question is allowed to percolate into the lower forms.

Another objection to the traditional approach is its strict adherence to chronology. Because of it, what is presented to any particular age-group is determined not by the intellectual and emotional capacity of the learner, but by the sequence of historical events. As was pointed out in the last chapter, to treat these events in the order in which they took place can be justified on account of the causal relationship between them, and is therefore logical.

However, when looked at from the point of view of the pupil and the stages of development through which he passes, the question takes on an entirely different aspect. What the traditional approach tries to do is to force him into a chronological strait-jacket which simply will not fit, and this places the teacher in an impossible situation. A few examples, taken from the syllabuses of secondary schools, will make the nature of this situation clear.

The first year usually includes a study of the Ancient Greeks and Romans. The teacher knows that what counts above everything else is the contribution the Greeks have made to Western Civilization in the realms of philosophy and the arts, and the ideas of government and law which the Romans have handed down to us. He also knows that if he attempts to interpret these to youngsters of eleven and twelve, he is undertaking something far above their level of understanding. But supposing that, instead of making the attempt, he were to concentrate on such things as the Battle of Marathon and Roman Villas, which are more within their mental grasp: that is all they would ever hear about the Ancient World at school, for in the strictly continuous course there is generally no provision for returning to a period once it has been dealt with.

Though it becomes less of an embarrassment as children grow older, the dilemma faces the teacher over and over again. In the second year, when it is the turn of the Middle Ages, the dilemma is caused by the conflict between Church and Crown, the following year by the spiritual awakening associated with the Renaissance and Reformation, and later by the constitutional developments leading to parliamentary democracy. Such situations are bound to arise as long as in this relentless forward march of time, chronology is the chief criterion. In each case, the choice lies between presenting the really important things at a time when the pupils are not ready for them, or banishing them from the syllabus once and for all.

This links up with another source of trouble, in that events which occurred at the same time in the past have to be dealt with at the same time at school. Frequently, no connection whatever exists between them, and if there is a connection, it is not made sufficiently clear. Facts which to the history specialist are part of a pattern, are to others often nothing but 'a series of more or less sanguinary events arbitrarily grouped under the names of persons who had to be identified with the assistance of numbers'.[1]

Happily, we no longer have the kind of textbook in which contemporaneous events jostled each other on the same pages in, to take an example, the chapter headed 'The Reign of George III'. There, hardly was there time for the unfortunate pupil to digest Pitt's India Act when it was the turn of Cartwright's power-loom. But before he became interested in the results of that invention the French Revolution broke out, which was the year after George III had his first attack of insanity. . . .

A partial remedy has been found by assembling allied topics into units and departing temporarily from the chronological arrangement. Helpful though this may be, it does not go to the root of the trouble. There is still too much switching from one topic to another, which leaves children confused and frustrated in their natural desire to see a

_____
[1] A. Bennet, *Clayhanger*, Book I, Ch. II.

story through to its conclusion. Thus the thread is lost. In addition to being constantly disturbed, the chronological narrative is dragged out for too long. When, at long last, the present is reached in the final year at school, it is not only the facts relating to the earlier historical periods which have been left behind but, which is more serious, the whole concept of a continuous development.

Not unexpectedly, the unsatisfactory nature of the syllabus has led to methods of presentation which are unsatisfactory too.

Although there are many variations of the manner in which the subject matter is traditionally presented, what characterizes the great majority of them is that, broadly speaking, the teacher is the mainspring of information and his medium the oral lesson. The teacher expounds and poses questions, and the pupils contribute by listening and answering questions. There are of course many other ways in which they acquire knowledge and make use of it, through reading books, writing essays, etc., but these do not alter the fact that they are assigned a secondary role.

The teacher who regards it as his duty to draw as much as is humanly possible from the vast fund of historical knowledge, can only hope to succeed if he gives a summarized version of it. In doing so, he is unable to avoid the use of such terms as 'balance of power', 'democracy', 'nationalism' and 'toleration'. To the initiated, these are generalizations which have an immediate significance, because an appreciation of the kind of instance for which they stand can be taken for granted. But without their concrete accompaniments, these terms have no meaning to children who lack the necessary background knowledge. They are abstractions which are, moreover, impersonal and for that reason alone lacking in appeal. For when historical characters are introduced into the lesson merely as pegs on which to hang ideas, how can they reach the status of real people in a child's mind?

Summaries have a useful function to perform—when there is something to summarize. But unless the body of the information has been previously digested, summaries are the very opposite of shortcuts to learning.

The process of compression also makes it inevitable that complex issues be simplified. If this is skilfully done, such issues can be made clear to all but the dullest, but the danger lies in oversimplification. The finished product may be perfectly intelligible but cannot any longer be described as historically accurate. The invention of so-called 'systems' (for example feudal, mercantile) has led to some unfortunate results in this respect.

Worse still, what emerges may be so disembodied that it does nothing to engender a spirit of inquiry. Pupils should be given the opportunity of finding out not only what things were, but why they were what they were. Data which have been processed are not conducive to making them reflect or evoking any kind of reaction on their part, such as expressing indignation or admiration.

Outlines result from the pressure under which the teacher has to hurry through the syllabus in a desperate attempt to keep abreast of it. He cannot really afford to expand on a point he has made, to follow it up or trace back in time, to pause and consolidate or establish comparisons. If he does any of these things, he runs the risk of not getting as far as the present time. His best prospect of success lies in keeping firmly in control of the subject matter, and the most efficient method of making certain that it is conveyed is to turn to a technique commonly identified with lecturing.

This technique is more suited to adult students. It causes evidence about the past, most of which has come down to us through the written word, to become even more verbal, and makes it remote and unreal in the eyes of those who are in no position to augment their knowledge from direct experience. Besides, the lecture is not so personal since it is addressed to an audience as a whole. It puts everyone on the same footing, being intended for the average rather than the more gifted at one end of the scale, or the less able at the other.

The straight talk also tends to cultivate the habit of sitting back and relying on the teacher as the dispenser of information. Young listeners are not able to concentrate on the spoken word for any length of time, however hard they may try, and they may not try because they have not experienced the sensation of being involved. When it is their turn to participate, their contribution easily becomes an exercise in memory, reproducing what was placed before them as something ready-made, rather than expressing something in which they shared.

It is by no means suggested that there is no place for oral instruction in the history lesson; but when constantly handling fresh material and presenting it in outline, the temptation to employ it to excess is almost irresistible. The corollary is to treat each lesson as self-contained. The danger of tying everything neatly into compact units is two-fold. It may lead to a standardization of teaching procedure (that is recapitulation—exposition—summing up); and since the length of a lesson is apt to dictate the shape into which the material is to be moulded, the notion may be conveyed that the past is a succession of isolated incidents.

Careering through the centuries may make sense to the teacher who, after all, is working to a plan, but not to his pupils in whose minds the superficial treatment leaves no clear impression. If something has been left out, they remain unaware of it. As far as they are able to judge, the course of events is followed systematically from beginning to end; and if by the time they leave school they come to the conclusion that the subject has been exhausted, it is scarcely their fault. How often one hears the remark, 'We "did" the Romans last term', as if the last word on the Romans had been said!

Apart from the teacher, the other main source of information accessible to pupils is the class textbook. Unless great care is taken, it too may help to perpetuate the delusion of comprehensiveness and, far from whetting their appetite, do the opposite.

To sum up: the conventional approach fails, and is bound to fail, on account of the incompatibility of the two premises on which it rests, that is, consecutiveness and completeness. Endeavouring to present the story of mankind in its entirety and, at the same time, to make it intelligible to children of school age is too ambitious a project for one subject in the curriculum to undertake. It does justice neither to history as a subject, nor to the children.

In view of what has been said it may seem astounding that the conventional syllabus should be still so widely followed. What is the explanation? There is little doubt that it would have been superseded by now if a more acceptable alternative could have been found. It is not that attempts have not been made to break with tradition. On the contrary, there are a number of departures which have been advocated from time to time. In all of them much of what is normally regarded as part and parcel of the history syllabus has been abandoned; and because the load has thus been lightened, departures from orthodox methods of presentation are made possible. This gives them an attractive look. Yet when they have been tried out in the classroom, there has usually been one, or more than one, factor which has disqualified them from being accepted as a satisfactory alternative to established practice.

Amongst the more important variants are the following:

One which is certainly not new is the so-called 'concentric' method, according to which the material is organized as though the learner were standing inside a series of ever-widening concentric circles. He progresses from the smaller to the larger circles as soon as his level of maturity permits it,

3

and whenever he does so, he is taken over the ground covered by its predecessor before being introduced to new material. Great care is therefore taken lest he should acquire information for which he is not ready. On the other hand if the method is followed to a logical conclusion, the same facts are met over and over again, all within the same chronological compass. To that the reaction of most people is one of utter boredom.

On an entirely different plane is 'local' history, in which prominence is given to the immediate environment and how it came to be what it is, as a microcosm of the national scene. Here it is possible to demonstrate, often in concrete terms, that the past does not only exist in books, and to use the familiar setting of the locality in order to introduce unfamiliar subject matter. The trouble is that so much depends on what a particular locality has to offer. Even if the scope is great, where does the boundary between local and national affairs lie, and can the latter be explained solely in terms of the former?

The 'biographical' approach to the teaching of history, on the other hand, seeks to illuminate the past by taking as the central theme the life stories of individual persons who were typical of their times or made a significant contribution to them. To the pupils, the appeal is immediate because of the human interest. To the teacher, the examples of the famous as well as infamous offer possibilities for demonstrating moral values. Whilst this may be accepted, a continuous story cannot easily be woven out of the lives of individual characters, no matter how many are assembled for the purpose. Moreover, the outcome is likely to be a distorted view of the course of events being fashioned entirely by individuals.

In another departure, the emphasis is on the ordinary people and how they lived, rather than on the outstanding people and what they did. This is known as 'social' history 'with the politics left out', as G. M. Trevelyan saw it.[1]

---

[1] Introduction to *English Social History*.

To focus the interest on the day-to-day problems with which 'folk like ourselves' had to cope has done much to throw into relevant perspective the former obsession with affairs at a governmental and national level. The disadvantage of singling out the social elements in history is that when human beings are lumped together into groups or classes, they thereby lose their identity and, to children, their fascination. Besides, the dynamic of action is totally lacking.

In what is known as 'social studies', the main criterion is contemporary relevance. This means that more recent developments and their bearing on the present-day society are in the foreground. Restricting the purpose of teaching history to preparing children for entry into their socio-economic environment has this to be said in favour of it: it entails the shedding of much of the remote and archaic material which has for so long cluttered up the syllabus, and at the same time underlines the importance of joining forces with other subjects in the curriculum for a common end. On the other hand, is it possible to define the body of knowledge which will meet the 'needs' of the present, and will it be of the kind to be relevant and appealing to any but adults?

Then there is the so-called 'lines of development' (or 'tunnel') approach. This entails the study of single themes, such as the story of transport or parliament, which are followed down the ages one by one. The order in which these are taken is determined by the pupils' intelligence and interest; and by concentrating on one theme at a time, the principle of continuity is clearly illustrated. It is, however, difficult to see how a theme can be isolated from the contemporary context and how the separate themes can be linked up in the end so as to form an integrated picture of the course of human development.

Attempts have also been made to explain current institutions and events in the first instance, and then to trace them back systematically through the centuries to their origins. Thus, the 'regressive' method of arranging the data follows the chronological principle. That is one of its strong points, as is the fact that the initial contact a child makes with history is through something he knows exists and matters. But it also means going from the complicated to the simple instead of, as is logical, the other way round; and the whole process runs counter to the natural order of things and can be very confusing even to adults.

In these short paragraphs it has not been possible to advance all the arguments in favour of or against the various departures from tradition. But what has been said is sufficient to make it understandable that teachers on the whole prefer, despite misgivings, to stick to the conventional outline plan. It is due not only to their natural conservatism, but the excessive zeal of the reformers and their refusal to make concessions.

To use horticultural language: those who press for reforms are right in claiming that the garden has become grossly overgrown, but the weeding they recommend is far too drastic. Some of the more valuable plants are irretrievably damaged in the process. Nor is the sowing any more successful, for many of the seeds fail to come up despite the attractive description on the packet. Not surprisingly, the hardy perennials reassert themselves triumphantly and the garden has changed little in appearance over the years.

Although the departures from tradition which have so far been mentioned follow different principles of selection, they have one thing in common: each is a study in development, showing how the present or a particular aspect of the present has grown out of the past into what it is today. In order to show this growth, it is traced step by step and the treatment thus follows the chronological pattern.

There is, however, an entirely different line of attack which does none of these things. This is the era approach.

4

The Era Approach

In the era approach the past is used for the purpose of making a study in comparison, the object being to find out where and in what ways the world of today differs from, or is similar to, the world of yesterday. This is done by extracting from the main stream of history certain periods of time. These 'eras', as they are called, are not connected with one another and cover each only a brief chronological span. Examples are the Roman Empire at its height, or Chaucer's England.

Each era is made the basis for a detailed inquiry into human life and institutions, so that a comprehensive and vivid picture of the past at the time in question may be obtained. In order to arrive at this picture, the inquiry is conducted from as many different angles as possible, to include political events, social customs, religious issues, the arts, communications, etc.

The responsibility for conducting the inquiry is handed over, as far as is practicable, to the pupils themselves. It can be undertaken at different levels and in different ways, and no one description can do justice to the diversity of classroom practice which is possible. For instance, each individual pupil may range over the era as a whole, or he may pick out a particular topic for special study. A common practice is a kind of compromise which looks something like this:

An era is divided into so-called 'fields of study' which between them cover it in all its aspects. The class is split up into the equivalent number of groups, each group being made responsible for a particular field of study. These fields are then explored by their respective groups, who find out all they can about them and produce a record of their findings.

As is the case with the other departures from tradition, the idea underlying this approach is not new. For example, a scheme in which the treatment of the subject matter was neither successive nor narrative was advocated by the German historian Biedermann in 1885. Biedermann proposed that pupils in secondary schools in Germany should not be required to pursue the course of their national history in its entirety, but should study it only at twelve key points which he selected with that intent and called 'Kulturbilder'.

It must also be made clear that the method of 'finding out' by the class, as opposed to 'giving out' by the teacher, is not the prerogative of this particular approach. It can be employed in any deviation from the conventional syllabus, when the selected material allows for a fuller treatment. What is unique is that this treatment is combined with the deliberate abandonment of the element of continuity.

In the pages which follow, an attempt is made to assess the value of the era approach, with special reference to the two fundamental respects in which it stands in direct contrast with more orthodox schemes of work: how the material is chosen and how it is used.

Making the past and not the present the starting point provides an effective antidote to the temptation to regard bygone ages merely as a series of stepping stones leading up to the present. Over-emphasis on the latter is apt to give rise to certain assumptions concerning the nature of history which are questionable. One of these is that the world of today is more readily understood than the world of yesterday. This is not necessarily the case, as the following arguments will show.

The first arises from the fact that we have a vested interest in the present. It is always easier to take a detached view of a distant scene of which we are the spectators than of the contemporary stage on which we are the actors. Secondly, we are never in a position to know as much about our own times as there is to be known, and any conclusions we draw cannot but be tentative. It is true that the evidence about the past is even more limited, but at least the limits are there for all to see. Finally, and this is the most striking argument, when we examine a particular aspect or event belonging to a former age, we know not only what happened then but what happened subsequently. This supreme advantage is denied to us when studying our own times, since it is not given to us to foretell the future.

These arguments lead to the further consideration that, whenever a sequence of events is followed straight through from beginning to end and the final outcome is known, there is a strong tendency to attach more weight to endeavours which were crowned with success than those which resulted in failure. From there it is but a short step to adopt a modernistic view of the past, by applying to it the standards of the present and judging it by those standards. This view easily leads to the assumptions that what is important to us today was of equal importance to our forefathers or, conversely, that if an issue is no longer a living issue, it is of no consequence and can therefore be minimized or even ignored.

The first assumption has been responsible for such fallacies as reading into the conflict between kings and barons in the thirteenth century a constitutional significance which it never possessed. And the second has sometimes resulted in the misrepresentation of those people whose actions were inspired primarily by religious motives, as was the case, for instance, in the seventeenth century.

Much of this kind of confusion of thought could be avoided if a clear distinction were maintained between progress and change. The historical process is essentially a process of change, and it is in the nature of change that it can be for the worse as well as for the better. But as soon as the notion of progress is introduced, subjectivity enters and it is taken for granted that there has been an advance or improvement. The past then no longer exists in its own right, but merely as a preparation for the present. There is the further danger that, if the march of events is looked upon as moving in an onward direction, the implication is that the rate of progress will be maintained.

Even without necessarily implying that there has been progress, there are those who would seek to explore the past not only in order thereby to understand better the world in which they live, but in order to adduce certain laws governing human life which are universal. The application of these laws, they claim, enables them to predict the future. Such is, for example, the Marxist interpretation of history. For this, strict adherence to chronology is essential: the present is regarded as having reached a certain stage in a course of evolution which, in view of its course so far, is predictable.

It is legitimate to use our knowledge derived from investigating the past for the purpose of dealing not only with the problems of the moment, but those of the future—they are really indistinguishable. No politician can afford not to do so. But it may be questioned whether the 'lessons' of history are meant to be rigidly applied; whether the historical process is in fact no more than an evolutionary process following a predetermined course over which we have no control; and even if it were, whether we are capable of ascertaining precisely at what stage we are at this moment.

Such speculations do not arise if the investigation is conducted from a neutral and disinterested point of view. This helps children to look upon their ancestors for what they were, different from us maybe, but not necessarily more simple, and does much to counteract a natural tendency to transport their present environment, because they are familiar with it, into the past. The reason for singling out particular eras for concentrated study is not their connection, either direct or indirect, with present-day institutions or values. The object, in the first instance, is to get as close as possible to things as they actually were and to examine them in their own right.

Supposing that what our young 'detectives' discover is quite different from what they are accustomed to from their everyday experience: this often makes a more effective start to explaining why there are these differences than if they had been led up to them by slow degrees. If, on the other hand, similarities are found, the discovery may be no less remarkable in view of the passage of time, and an explanation is called for. In either case the technique is one of direct comparison.

Applying, as it were, a magnifying glass to a period of life remote from our own requires an effort in imagination and provides the sensation of entering into the spirit of another age. As we have seen, it is hardly possible to achieve this along conventional lines since the fast pace precludes giving concrete examples and enlarging on them, which is so essential for illuminating the past and bringing it to life in the minds of children. To them, everything seems twice removed from reality: in space as well as in time. This is one of the difficulties which is not met, to the same extent, in any other subject.

It is true that details are, in themselves, often trivial and that children have an exasperating habit of seizing upon trivialities. However, need this alarm us as long as details are regarded not as an end, but as a device for lending a sense of reality to the study of the past? And if, by way of illustration, all a pupil remembers of the execution of Charles I is that he wore an extra shirt in case he should be thought to be trembling with fear: is this not preferable to knowing merely the year of his death, which may well be the case if he has been taught by summaries? On the contrary, it will help him not to forget the date if he is anything like Sissy Jupe, of whom Dickens wrote that she was 'extremely slow in the acquisition of dates, unless some pitiful incident happened to be connected therewith'.[1]

So that generalizations can be made and inferences drawn, the starting point must always be the particular, and this is, of course, the way in which anyone undertaking research sets about his business. The application to detail is necessary not only in order to do justice to history as a subject, but to fill a psychological need. It satisfies a child's natural curiosity and confronts him with something manageable which, when he has mastered it, gives a sense of satisfaction and achievement. In his own particular field he will be the acknowledged authority, and his class-mates will respect him as such.

If what has been mastered in terms of area of knowledge is not so extensive, it is as well to remind ourselves that however much we may learn about the past, it is insignificant in comparison to what there is to be known. The past is inexhaustible, but if we throw out a challenge to probe it further and that challenge is accepted, we shall not have failed.

The treatment in depth is directed not merely to one or two isolated topics—a religious issue here, an architectural item there, as so often is the case—but to all the manifold aspects which together constitute an age and how these affect one another. Stretching, as it were, right across the age involves going far beyond the boundaries of what is normally regarded as the province of history in the school curriculum. Here history can play a unique part in helping to bridge the gaps which, unhappily, exist between one department and another. The following examples will show where links can, and indeed must, be forged.

English literature takes children to an important source of our knowledge of former times, whether the account be documentary, such as *The Letters of Private Wheeler*, or

[1] *Hard Times*, Ch. 9.

fictitional, as *Mary Barton*. Through these an authentic and vivid picture is obtained of life in the army and of the conditions of the working classes in the early part of the nineteenth century, which no textbook account can hope to equal. A gate to the understanding of the later Middle Ages, on the other hand, is thrown open by the Prologue to Chaucer's *Canterbury Tales*.[1]

Geography provides another obvious example, since at every turn man's dealings with his fellow-men and his endeavours to master his environment have been influenced by the economic resources of the earth and its physical features. Thus Hereward the Wake's spectacular resistance to William I can only be properly explained if it is remembered that the Isle of Ely was once a real island.

Again, there is much in history which does not make sense if the religious implications underlying an issue are ignored or an understanding of them is taken for granted. Thus when dealing with the events resulting from the revolt against the Established Church in the seventeenth century, it is necessary to know something of the articles of the Church to which exception was taken.

Regarding the Sciences, reference need be made only to the technical inventions and scientific discoveries which heralded the so-called 'Industrial Revolution'. James Watt and Thomas Telford become more than names in a list of inventors, as soon as the factors involved in translating steam into power or constructing a bridge on the suspension principle are explained in detail.

Further instances could be drawn from the more practical subjects, such as woodwork, art and needlework, which can do so much to make the past more realistic by supplementing the written word. But enough has been said to draw attention to the many benefits an historical inquiry will reap through being more closely associated with other subjects in the curriculum, and they too stand to gain from

[1] See Era No. 9 in Appendix 1.

such an association. A mutual enrichment will, however, take place only on the condition that a generous amount of time is lavished on the inquiry.

Taking a broad view also goes some way towards preserving the unity which permeates the whole body of historical knowledge, yet tends to be disrupted by the exigencies of the school timetable. But when a set task is carried over from one lesson into the next, it does not matter to the same extent if there are several days between them. The single lesson then loses its dominating character; it is treated merely as a link in a chain, and the length of the chain is determined by the task in hand.

The task itself is designed to appeal to children because there is a spice of adventure about it. It is not for the teacher to start from date x and arrive at date y—both arbitrary in the eyes of the uninitiated—but for the children to embark on a fact-finding mission by, say, imagining themselves back in the days of King Alfred. This is something they can readily understand, and, coupled with the knowledge that it is they who are going to do the finding out, is more likely to evoke an enthusiastic response than a continuation of a weary journey through a seemingly endless and unrelated sequence of events, in which they are passengers. As in any other branch of learning, history will yield meaningful answers only if definite questions are put to it in the first place. In other words, the inquirer must know what he is looking for.

Turning now to the manner in which the inquiry is carried out, we find that it affords an excellent medium for the acquisition of three important skills: those of knowing how to search for information; how to interpret it; and how to express it.

The first of these skills brings children into contact with reference books and provides training in handling them. Here their passion for collecting—by no means confined to material objects—can be enlisted as a powerful ally. Since what they are looking for is of a specific nature, a great many sources have to be consulted other than the single textbook. This leads to some important discoveries: that generally more books than one have been written on the same subject; that, apart from the title, they may have little in common; and that however authoritative they may be, none of them can be described as exhaustive.

During the course of their inquiry, children usually read far more than is expected of them, and in this way the habit of supplementary reading is encouraged and much peripheral information gleaned. This information may be 'useless' for the moment, but is likely to stimulate interest and widen their horizon. Seen in that light, the time spent on the perusal of an entire chapter in order to unearth one single item is well rewarded.

Reading with discrimination comes somewhat later, when the startling and sometimes disconcerting discovery is made that, whilst facts as such cannot be altered, it is legitimate for writers to differ in their interpretation of these facts. Only if more than one book on the same subject is consulted, can this be brought out.

Finding out what the appropriate reference works are is a preliminary to learning how to utilize the information they offer. This consists not merely of collecting and reproducing, but necessitates the sorting out of relevant from irrelevant material and rearranging the former. In this connection, the making of notes acts as an invaluable discipline for clear and orderly thinking, besides serving as an aid to memory, and enables the teacher to check on what has been read and whether it has been understood.

To select what is useful for a particular purpose, and to reject what is not, requires considerable thought and judgment. These faculties cannot be trained if the notes are dictated by the teacher, or if they are summarized by the class from the textbook which, in itself, is already a summary.

But they can be trained if the nature of the task is such that it acts as a challenge to the child to think for himself and attempt to arrive at conclusions of his own, and, if difficulties are encountered, he is allowed to grapple with them and learns to overcome them.

There is, finally, ample scope for self-expression through a variety of media. The most commonly used medium for recording a result is the written account, which can be fitted in conveniently both with the coverage of the textbook and the development of a theme by the teacher in his oral exposition. It should, however, not be the sole medium, for formal writing is not the most natural form of expression— at any rate, with younger or less able children—and is apt to be reproductive rather than creative.

There are other, often more striking forms to which boys and girls will resort quite spontaneously when an interest has been allowed to build up over a period of time. One example is acting. This helps to recapture the spirit of the times in a way that few other media can and provides an admirable exercise in imagination, particularly if the scene or play has been made up by the pupils themselves. It is then a genuine reflection of the impression gained from consulting books of reference. Such an exercise also brings home the need for strict historical accuracy and attention to detail (regarding costume, idiom, etc.), and the whole production can leave a deep and lasting impression in young minds.

Models provide another example. What a Norman castle was like can be explained in so many words; a drawing will make it clearer; but undoubtedly the most effective way of making it real in a child's mind is to produce a scale model of a castle.

Other media include the making of illustrations and drawing of charts, all of which are creative and provide scope for expression along individual lines, as well as scope for social training. From the point of view of both teacher and taught, practical activity of this kind makes a welcome change from the routine of reading and writing which occupies so much of their time at school. The finished product may well leave something to be desired, but more often than not, this is outweighed by the satisfaction a child obtains from the fact that a particular piece of work is his own. From the recognition he receives and sense of achievement he experiences can spring self-confidence.

All this has long been accepted. Why is it, then, that not more opportunities are offered in the history lesson for giving training in the skills of searching for information, interpreting it and expressing it? The answer is that to develop them takes time and, with teachers being haunted by the spectre of falling behind in the annual race on the chronological cinder-track, time is the enemy of the conventional approach.

Hence pupils are, as a rule, brought up in close dependence on the teacher and the textbook until they reach the sixth form, when all of a sudden they are presumed to be capable of producing work for themselves. There is no reason why they should not be able to do so well before the age of sixteen, and an era study can help to bring this about, since practice in acquiring the above-mentioned skills is given much earlier than is normally the case. If mistakes are made—and no problem can be solved without making allowances for that—there is more than one chance to rectify and profit from them.

It is always tempting to circumscribe carefully a set piece of work and the method by which it is to be undertaken, but a teacher can discover a great deal about his pupils, and they about themselves, if permitted greater freedom. For what is produced is not as uniform as it tends to be when all are engaged in the same task, at the same time. This has two advantages: it enables the individual to proceed at his own pace, and allows his work to be guided by his own personal interests.

The very unpredictability of the outcome, disconcerting as at times it may be, gives an insight into a child's mind, his inclinations and abilities, as no amount of prescribed work will do. In the course of the undertaking it is not only existing interests which are utilized and developed, but frequently a new interest is awakened in something which is not usually part of a history lesson, such as brass rubbings, coins or heraldry, which may last throughout life.

If the enterprise is carried out by the class operating in groups (as described in Chapters 6 and 7), there are a number of advantages arising from such an arrangement which are obvious to anyone with experience of group work. The smaller the unit to which a pupil belongs, the less likelihood there is of his remaining inactive, and the more scope there is for him to make his way in accordance with his capacity and for the teacher to give him personal attention and encouragement. As regards the size of the enterprise, the fact that it is tackled simultaneously from different angles means that, added together, more is accomplished than is ordinarily possible.

The resources of a group are, of course, much superior to those of the individual members of whom it is composed; and this, together with the spirit which emanates from a corporate effort, can lead to results of which an individual is often incapable if left to himself, or for which he has no inclination if one of a large number. Finally, there is a good prospect that through the experience of striving for a common end, habits of co-operation may be developed.

At first sight, the above arguments appear to build up to a powerful case for replacing the orthodox approach to the teaching of history by a system of era studies. It would, however, be surprising if the latter did not have its drawbacks too, and anyone contemplating adopting such a system would be well advised to examine the arguments on the other side.

5

Disadvantages of the Era Approach

The discussion which follows is as much concerned with the disadvantages at a theoretical level, as with the sort of difficulty which is encountered when the era concept is applied in the classroom. As is always the case, the practice throws fresh light on the theory, and what faults may be said to be inherent in the concept cannot be readily separated from the faults which develop when the concept is translated into action.

Let us begin with the choice of historical material. Here it may be said straight away that, whereas the outline approach was rightly criticized for sacrificing the needs of the pupils on the altar of chronology, it can be claimed with equal justification that the era approach offers its victims on the altar of thoroughness.

The aim, after all, is to create an all-round impression of an age, and to be consistent with that aim presupposes that no essential aspect be omitted. Followed to its logical conclusion, this is bound to embrace many issues which are too complex or advanced for children to understand, and thus offends against one of the fundamental principles in all teaching, that the material should always be matched with their interests and abilities.

The dangers of making the needs of the present the sole criterion have previously been noted. But does it follow that we must make the age which is being studied the basis of selection, and allow ourselves to be guided by nothing but what was of concern to our forefathers? No reconstruction

4
49

of the fifteenth century is complete without an account of the conflict between the Yorkists and Lancastrians, but that hardly provides adequate grounds for inflicting its vicissitudes on youngsters of thirteen or fourteen.

In an effort to avoid the pitfalls of looking back over the centuries through contemporary spectacles, the adherent of the era approach is apt to go to the opposite extreme and to bury his head in the sands of the past. Studying the past 'for its own sake' does not necessarily lead to an understanding of it, nor does it lead to an understanding of the present which must always be the ultimate goal of learning about history. Neither makes sense unless it is brought into relationship with the other, for just as the past is capable of illuminating the present, it has in itself no relevance unless it is interpreted in the light of today.

Only too easily, the endeavour of arriving at an objective picture of things 'as they were' becomes an obsession, so that the next step is omitted, which is to draw parallels or point out contrasts between the world of our forefathers and the world in which we live. Without this step, there can be no living connection between them.

There is a corollary of this which is also apt to be overlooked. If one of the objectives of teaching the subject is to enable children to make judgments of human conduct, the exercise in comparison must be extended so as to include questions relating to moral issues. Otherwise they may become merely interested onlookers and get into the habit of accepting differences, when they meet them, uncritically and of regarding values as being relative.

It is true, of course, that the standards of today may not be the standards of tomorrow, but this does not absolve the present generation from having standards and from striving after reform and progress. Children have a quick sense of justice and should not feel discouraged from venturing an opinion on, say, the treatment of slaves in the eighteenth century, just because by eighteenth-century standards it was part of the accepted order to treat slaves like cattle. In short, there is a real danger that detachment may lead to indifference and the cultivation of a false reverence for anything which bears the label 'historical'.

All the above faults stem, at bottom, from the break with continuity which is so absolute that there is no hope of placing an era into a historical perspective. Young children have very little experience of time and for that reason they are not conscious of it. To them the past is as definite as the present—a thing either *was* or *is*—and they find it difficult to comprehend that an event may have occurred as little as ten, or as many as a thousand years ago. It is important that this comprehension should be developed as early as possible, since two conditions are necessary before a fact can qualify as being historical: it must be shown to have occurred at a certain place, and at a certain time. Otherwise it belongs to the province of fiction, not history. A time sense is, therefore, indispensable if an ordered view of the past is to be taken.

Formerly a misguided trust was put in the soul-destroying practice of memorizing whole lists of dates. But to go to the opposite extreme and neglect dates altogether, just because within the narrow chronological confines of an era they are of less consequence, is no less a mistake. It deprives us of an essential tool, for dates provide a yardstick by which the conditions and events of former ages can be given a place in time, and by which they can be arranged in the order in which they belong and their duration measured.

It is questionable, to say the least, whether proceeding by eras, spaced as they are at irregular intervals in time, or taken altogether out of their chronological sequence, makes any positive contribution to solving our problem. It is more likely to leave children with the impression that history is like a kaleidoscope in which none of the pretty patterns has a bearing on any other.

Equally serious is the failure to impart the idea of evolution and the essential continuity of one thing growing out of another and leading into the next. Facts do not only have a place in time, but are also related in time. According to the era concept, however, they may well be thought static since each era is treated as though it were self-contained, with a gap of 50, 100 or even 200 years between one and the next. No sooner has the picture of one era been built up, when a jump is made and another is started which has no apparent connection with the previous one.

Such a procedure is admirable from the point of view of demonstrating that change is the life-blood of history, but does nothing to answer the question: what makes for change? To establish differences between any two given points in time is not enough. Differences have their causes, and in order to account for these, reference must be made to what happened in the interval. Likewise, the significance of an action cannot be assessed if no consideration is given to the consequences arising from the action, long-term as well as immediate. There is, in short, a continuum which is broken only at a heavy price.

Whatever else a child may gain from an intensive study of a limited number of significant epochs, he is not thereby helped to acquire an attitude towards the concept of growth and development. If the emphasis is on the social aspects of man's past, the disruption in continuity may not be so serious. It was, in fact, the technique successfully employed by G. M. Trevelyan who set out to 'tell the story as life is presented on the stage, that is to say by a series of scenes divided by intervals of time'.[1] But political, legal and military matters, to mention just a few, cannot be made intelligible if treated solely in this manner.

In our discussion of the weaknesses of the era approach so far, it has been taken for granted that fitting all the parti-

---

[1] Introduction to *English Social History*.

culars into a recognizable pattern creates no difficulties and that the object of painting a complete picture of a bygone age can, therefore, be realized. Is that in fact possible? Let us first take the case of each individual pupil attempting to cover an era as a whole. This course is not likely to commend itself for the following reasons:

In the first place, if all are tackling the same ground simultaneously the problem of supplying adequate source material is aggravated. Secondly, the presentation of the information is bound to be more stereotyped, since the amount is so considerable as to make it almost impossible to present it in other than written form. But, most important of all, the ground is too extensive to allow for treatment in depth, and if the image thus obtained is a superficial one it is no improvement on more traditional ways of teaching the subject.

Let us assume, on the other hand, that the work has been divided up and the pupils, operating either individually or in groups, have satisfactorily covered their respective fields of study. To leave matters there and pass on to the next era would not only be a cause for regret, but a major error. For, all the time that Andrew has been engaged in a particular piece of work in one corner of the classroom, David, in another, has been busy doing something else, and it is natural that they should be curious about each other's efforts and want to compare notes.

There is an even more compelling reason for not regarding an era study as completed at, what is surely, a crucial moment. Unless all the various findings are brought together and co-ordinated, the whole point of the initial inquiry will have been missed: to give to every single member of the class a vision of a certain period of the past. For what is the position? Each has enough fuel to light up his particular corner, but the main expanse of the territory to be explored will remain shrouded in darkness as before. This is why it is fatal to abandon the undertaking before the separate elements have been formed into a connected whole.

It was contended earlier that a sure grasp of a limited portion of knowledge was more valuable than a hazy notion extending over a wide area. If the question concerned only factual knowledge and nothing else, the comparative lack of it regarding the non-explored fields of study need cause no alarm. One shaft of light, though it be directed at only a section of an age, can do much to illuminate the age, provided one essential condition is fulfilled: that it is related to the age as a whole.

From his lofty height, the teacher enjoys a panoramic view of the unfolding of the past and stands in no danger of losing sight of the relationship. A child's vision, by contrast, is limited and he may well miss completely the significance of his particular contribution. In the glow following the successful completion of individual assignments, this is often forgotton.

We have now arrived at the other main distinguishing feature of the approach, which is the emphasis on pupil activity. The comments which follow apply to all age groups, but more especially to younger than to older pupils.

By placing the responsibility for the undertaking almost entirely on their shoulders, a strain is imposed which may well be too great. For intelligent research is an art which demands more than a certain degree of technical competence. It also demands on the part of the researcher a mature attitude of mind, without which he will fail to apply properly the tools with which he has been issued and, amongst a welter of detail, lose sight of the object altogether.

Children—and many adults too—tend to assemble data mechanically if left to themselves, such data often being either irrelevant or unrelated, or gaze at illustrations without realizing their meaning. The books at their disposal are, after all, addressed to an impersonal reader and, however well they may have been written or illustrated, cannot be expected to give an answer to every question or anticipate every problem which the individual reader may encounter. The principles underlying the so-called 'activity' methods are sound enough, but it must not be taken for granted that when youngsters bury their noses in books or wield paintbrush and scissors, they are *ipso facto* undergoing an educational experience.

It is not only that they lack the necessary maturity, but in history, unlike the natural sciences, the evidence is never such that it leads to certainties. Facts cannot be isolated from their significance and that is why history is not an objective study. It is very largely based on contemporary accounts by writers who reported in the context of their particular situations—compare Burke's version of the French Revolution with that of Paine. And modern historians who use these accounts as sources cannot remain unbiased, try as they may, since they have to select from contemporary evidence and then interpret it.

The most that can be said is that children can be shown how to verify their findings as far as they relate to factual matters, and they may even be encouraged to make deductions of their own from these findings. But what they are incapable of doing by themselves is to assess the validity of their deductions. It is here that they need most help, for as Bertrand Russell has pointed out, 'One of the most important parts of education, and one of the most neglected, is that which teaches how to reach true conclusions on insufficient data . . . all success in practical life depends upon ability to perform this apparently impossible feat.'[1]

As in all things, a balanced view must be taken. In this case, the balance is between a straight narrative which is concerned with general trends and delivered by the teacher, and an independent search aimed at the particular and carried out by the children. If, traditionally, the scales have been weighted in favour of the former, the balance is not restored by going to the other extreme.

[1] *Education and the Social Order*, Ch. XV.

No book can enliven the past and communicate an enthusiasm about it as the teacher can through the force of his personality and directness of his approach. If it is well delivered, a good story—and what subject other than English contains such wealth?—always makes a deeper impression than it does in print, and a class which listens spell-bound is anything but inactive.

It is the teacher too who will help his pupils to recognize, and to grapple with, the many live issues with which history is shot through. This is a responsibility which he must not evade. For in everyday life they are continually required to make decisions and act in the light of these, and to treat their work in class merely as an exercise in recording and analysing is to divorce history from life. The trial of Warren Hastings, for instance, raises questions which are as relevant today as they were 200 years ago, but one would not expect to find a discussion of them in a book of reference.

All this goes to show that the abuses to which the conventional approach lays itself open must not blind us to the virtues of the class lesson conducted by oral means, without which the history period can be as arid as the one-sided display of the teacher delivering his discourse. The latter is far from being the only means of imparting information. A more appropriate way, with young people at any rate, is to employ the question-and-answer technique, in which known data are developed with the object of eliciting new facts and ideas from the children themselves. However, no further amplification is necessary to remind ourselves of the vital part the teacher can, and must, play if they are to obtain the maximum benefit from their contact with the past.

Even with the teacher restored to his rightful place, there remain a number of difficulties of a purely practical nature. The first difficulty is one which does not exist when the general textbook answers the need for supporting reading material. But here books are wanted which deal with selected topics in some detail, and at the same time impart the information in such a way that children can readily understand it.

Two pertinent questions may be asked: Are books which meet these special requirements available? If so, since the whole class will be using them simultaneously, have the schools the required financial resources to purchase copies in sufficient quantities to go round? Lack of suitable source material may easily wreck the whole undertaking, and if it cannot be done well, it is best not to attempt it at all.

Similar troubles may be experienced if too much trust is placed in pictorial illustrations. Reproductions of contemporary pictures are valuable because they bear the stamp of authenticity, but are apt to be obscure. Line drawings, on the other hand, are distinct and to the point but not always reliable.

As for preparing and marshalling the various items of equipment, this may put the teacher to a good deal of extra trouble. Most of it has to be done out of school hours, and not everyone will feel that he can afford the time and, quite possibly, expense.

Once the investigation is under way, there are the usual organizational snags with which anyone with experience of class projects is only too familiar. They arise from supervising simultaneously the work of (more or less willing) pupils, who are on different assignments and at different stages of progress—all of which necessitate that the teacher should be in thirty or forty places at once, a model of patience, a living encyclopaedia and an expert at every craft.

At those times the classroom becomes a reading room, workshop and stage all rolled into one. Some children are poring over books, while others are moving about arranging a wall display or, more alarmingly still, rehearsing a playlet, and it does not require much imagination to picture the chaos that can so easily ensue. . . .

57

It will be evident from the foregoing that despite some outstanding merits, teaching by eras as it has been described suffers from too many drawbacks to be recommended as a satisfactory alternative to the traditional general survey. In common with other major departures from convention, it is the victim of its own extremism, which explains why it has hitherto made relatively little impact on the schools. Must it, therefore, be rejected out of hand? That does by no means follow, provided certain measures are taken to meet the criticisms which have been levelled against it.

The principles on which these measures are to be based will by now be clear. They may be summarized as follows:

1. The study of an era must be carried out in such a way that a pupil becomes *au fait* with more than his own contribution.

2. To establish an era in its own right is not enough; it needs to be viewed in its own historical context, as well as that of the present day.

3. Both in developing the skills demanded by the task and in seeing the wider implications, a pupil requires more help than he usually receives.

4. For this help he will look to the teacher, who must be prepared to take upon himself a difficult role, that of intermediary.

In the next two chapters, a step by step account is given of the application of the approach in relation to a particular era. Incorporated into the account are a number of modifications which many teachers, who are attracted by the approach, have successfully adopted. The modifications apply as much to the subject matter selected for study as to the way in which it is handled. For the sake of clarity, only one procedure is followed—that of pupils working on group (rather than individual) assignments.

6

The Era Approach in Action (I):
Preparation and Planning

(*a*) CHOOSING AN ERA

The first concern is with deciding which eras are to be
studied in detail. Since the underlying purpose is to compare the past with the present with the intention of helping
to bring about a better understanding of the latter, it could
be argued that any period of the past can be made to serve
this purpose. This is true, but does not absolve the teacher
from making a choice, and at once all the fundamental
issues pertaining to the selection of historical material are
raised. With these issues every teacher of history is brought
face to face, no matter which particular line of approach
he favours, and since they were fully discussed in the opening
chapter it is not proposed to go into them again. Apart
from the more fundamental considerations, the choice
depends on the answers to a number of related questions.

The first of these questions refers to the time devoted to
the study of one era. This varies in practice and no hard
and fast rules can be laid down, with the proviso that
the ground must always be explored thoroughly. Speaking
very generally, on the assumption that no more than two
to three lessons a week are allocated to history, it is hardly
possible to do justice to an era in less than six weeks. On
the other hand, it is unlikely to exceed a term.

In schools in which pupils are expected to do homework,
the duration may be shorter, for much of the preliminary
reading can be continued outside school hours. Then, also,
much of the writing up of notes or work connected with

the building of models can be done, all of which is time-consuming. It will make an appreciable difference, too, if the liaison with other subjects in the curriculum is such that some of the work is carried out in their time, particularly if the undertaking is of an ambitious nature.

The duration of one complete study is conditional also on the total number of eras included in the syllabus, and this in turn depends on their range in terms of both time and space. For example, it is probably desirable, and certainly legitimate, to place a liberal interpretation on Athens in the fifth century and to overstep the limits of the hundred-year period, as well as cross the physical boundaries of the City State. But supposing the object were to find out all about the Regency period, it would not be difficult to muster enough material at home without having to look further afield.

Such limits as are imposed by dates are clearly arbitrary and it is best to regard an era as a flexible unit. The main thing is to keep a sense of balance. If the era is too long, a detailed treatment of it becomes an impossibility. If it is too short, justice can scarcely be done to the element of continuity. With the advent of modern times, however, it is true to say that the chronological range becomes smaller and smaller, and so do the intervals between eras. On the occasions that different parts of the world are explored, the eras may overlap or run parallel.

In some schools it is customary to attempt a substantial number of short studies following each other in rapid succession. In others, teachers prefer these studies to be on a large scale, in which case the total number of eras in the syllabus will be proportionately less.[1]

(b) PARTITIONING THE ERA

How is the inquiry to be undertaken by the class? As we saw earlier, no matter what procedure is adopted, it is

[1] For a specimen syllabus, see Appendix 1.

fraught with difficulties. On balance, some form of specialization seems preferable, provided that the consequences are squarely faced. Hence having chosen an era, the next step is, as it were, to take it to pieces.

The Elizabethan Age has for long been a favourite with teachers and pupils alike and will be taken as an example. It has been divided into six fields of study, and the topics which are listed under each heading give an indication as to the ground each field is meant to cover.

(1) *Houses and Domestic Life*

Architecture; Halls and hovels; Furniture and furnishing; Gardens; Food and drink; Banquets; Smoking; Clothes; Fashions; Family life; Education.

(2) *Exploration and Warfare*

Ships; Voyages of discovery; Drake and the 'sea-dogs'; Trade; Sir Walter Raleigh and Virginia; Sailors and soldiers; Weapons; The Netherlands; War with Spain; The Armada.

(3) *Religion and Rebellions*

The Church Settlement; The Counter-Reformation; Philip II; Edmund Campion; Mary Queen of Scots; John Knox; Puritans; Huguenots; Henry IV; The Irish Rebellion.

(4) *Town and Country*

London; City Companies; Shops; The woollen industry; Apprentices; Farming; Enclosures; 'Sturdy beggars'; The Poor Law; Roads; Inns; Merchants; Fairs and markets.

(5) *Arts and Pastimes*

Shakespeare and other writers; The Globe Theatre; Plays and masques; Musical instruments; Madrigals; Dancing; Hawking and other sports; Bear gardens and cock fighting; Feasts and festivals.

(6) *Government and Institutions*

> Queen Elizabeth; The Queen's favourites; The royal household; The Court; Royal progresses; The Queen's councillors; Parliament; Justices of the Peace; Punishments.

It must be stressed that there is nothing doctrinaire about the above classification. For instance, some people will prefer to separate *Town* and *Country*, and others will have their reservations about keeping numbers 2 and 3 apart. Nor is the list of topics intended to be exhaustive. The grounds on which any such list is made up, and the level and extent to which each topic is explored, are individual and depend on the age and ability range of the children, and much else besides. The aim is to strike a balance between importance and interest. But since neither of these is an absolute concept, it is certain that no divisions and subdivisions would ever meet with unanimous approval, even if all the circumstances were identical.

Again, there are bound to be differences of opinion regarding the number of fields of study into which an era is to be partitioned, in view of the fact that, in our example, the work of exploring them will be carried out by the pupils working in groups. The number of groups is determined by the number of fields, which means that the more groups there are, the fewer pupils there will be in each.

There is much to be said for the effectiveness of small 'research units'. As against this, attention must be drawn to a problem which is not encountered until later on: how to correlate the various assignments. The greater their number, the greater the degree of specialization by each group, and the harder it is to achieve this correlation. For that reason, it may be advisable not to have too many groups, particularly when dealing with younger children.

In a sense, fields of study may be likened to pieces in a jig-saw puzzle. What matters is that together they should make up a complete picture, and the number of pieces and the size of them are subordinate to this object. It is, however, worth remembering that the smaller a piece is, the smaller the area it covers and the more difficult it is to locate its proper place.

In other respects the analogy is totally false, for whereas one piece of a jig-saw puzzle makes no sense by itself, it is essential that a field of study should do so, though it represents but a fragment of an age. Moreover, a jig-saw piece only fits in one place, whereas a field of study, because it concerns people, is anything but static.

From the start the aim should be to involve the pupils as closely as possible with the job in hand. This aim is not easily achieved, since the territory to be surveyed is completely strange to them and the events of the past cannot be conjured up by an exercise of the imagination.

Without question, the teacher is in the best position to decide on the extent of an era and to map out its constituent parts. But he must be careful not to go to the extremes of making a bald announcement, giving headings and sub-headings and issuing precise instructions as to the manner in which to proceed. Such a course of action would be a mistake psychologically, for children are always more eager to tackle a piece of work if they can be made to feel that the initiative in launching it was theirs.

In fact, it should not be outside their compass to appreciate the fact that their forefathers, no matter at what period of history they lived, were faced with the same kinds of problems: how to dress and procure food for themselves, how to earn their living and spend their leisure hours, and how to move from one place to another. The conflict between ruler and ruled and between nation and nation, too, is a perennial one. By skilful questioning many topics can be elicited—at least as far as the general social background of an era is concerned—and allied topics joined up in order to form fields of study. After a time there emerges what might almost be described as a formula which, with suitable modifications, can be applied over and over again.

At all times it will be found helpful if the material is so planned as to establish as many points of contact between the separate fields as possible. A fair amount of overlapping is not only inevitable but desirable, *Religion and Rebellions* and *Exploration and Warfare* being obvious examples in the Elizabethan scheme. The important thing to remember is that, whatever lines of division are adopted, they cannot but be artificial, and are in fact only temporary. They are merely intended to make the subsequent task, that of arriving at the picture of an era as a whole, a manageable one.

This last statement must be qualified. There are features relating to every age which by their nature are beyond the pupils' mental reach. It would be disastrous to include these merely for the sake of completeness, in order to justify the claim that the age has been traversed in its entirety. On the contrary, the limitations of young minds must be clearly recognized, as regards the ability both to understand complexities of a specific nature and to achieve a balanced overall view.

Having therefore selected from the main course of historical events a particular portion for close inspection, the teacher must not hesitate to omit further anything that is plainly unsuited. Whilst the obtaining of a comprehensive view of certain stretches of time remains the prime object, the term 'comprehensive' must be relative to a child's level of vision. Here, then, is our first inroad into the logical structure of the era approach.

(*c*) ASSEMBLING SOURCES AND MATERIALS

The need for discrimination will exert a powerful influence on the task of taking stock of all the sources to which reference has to be made and, if necessary, of adding to them. Adequate source material is essential for an undertaking of this kind, which relies on detailed information being readily available to the children pursuing their various inquiries. All this requires careful planning, and it may well be that a shortage of certain indispensable reference material will cause the original list of topics comprising a field of study to be revised.

Amongst the sources from which the information can be obtained are, first and foremost, books. Those which belong to the category of reference rather than textbooks will be found more helpful, for if the class textbook follows the conventional pattern, it is likely to embrace the entire Tudor and Stuart period in one volume.[1]

Clearly, a work which deals exclusively with the reign of Queen Elizabeth I is preferable, particularly if it specializes in a certain aspect of the time, such as voyages of exploration. Books which trace particular topics through the ages will also be useful; one on costumes, for instance, is bound to have several pages devoted to the sixteenth century, where members of Group I will find all they want to know about ruffs and farthingales. Finally, the standard encyclopaedias are an invaluable standby.

Many such books can be found in the library of any school, but it is more than likely that the existing stock will have to be supplemented by going outside the school, through the offices of the City or County Library and other reference libraries. Pupils are sometimes able to help by raiding the shelves of their parents or relations, and no doubt the teacher has his personal collection to draw on.

Illustrations, too, provide a mine of information, whether they be reproductions of contemporary drawings or, what may be better, line-drawings based on the former. Most of the above-mentioned books will contain pictures, diagrams or maps. This applies to textbooks too, and educational

[1] For series of reference books, see Appendix 2.

publishers have not been slow to appreciate the importance of the visual approach. Several pictorial source books, which carry only short descriptive passages, have been produced, and historical atlases, sketchmap histories and wall charts, etc. are available in increasing numbers.

Of more limited use, but worth exploring, are the sets of postcards, transparencies and guides which can be purchased from museums and art galleries. There are also several periodicals entirely devoted to history, and these frequently contain articles and illustrations which are not readily obtainable elsewhere. In fact, pictures of historical interest can sometimes be found in the most unexpected quarters, even in the daily paper or popular magazine, and with a little determination it should not be long before a respectable collection is built up.

Other fruitful sources must not be overlooked. Some schools may be so fortunate as to be situated in a district in which visible memorials of Tudor times still exist: a white-and-black timber-framed house, for instance, or a church containing monuments set into the wall which can be visited by the groups in the course of their inquiries. Elsewhere, it will be possible to arrange an outing to a nearby museum or country house where, perhaps, examples of Elizabethan tapestry, miniatures, musical instruments or pieces of wrought iron work are on display.

Enough has been said to give an indication of the extensive range of sources that are waiting to be tapped, in and outside the classroom. How many are taken advantage of depends on local conditions; but it also depends to no small degree on the trouble to which one is prepared to go.

No difficulty should be experienced in assembling the necessary working materials. These comprise, in the first instance, paper: scrap paper for taking down rough notes; file paper for writing up notes; drawing paper for illustrations; cartridge paper for making posters; tracing paper; blotting paper—in fact paper of almost any kind or description.

Then there are the tools essential for writing and drawing: pens, pencils, crayons, brushes, Indian ink, paints, water colours, etc. In addition, depending on what form the final reports by the pupils are going to take, provision will have to be made for some or all of the following to be available: cardboard, hardboard, papier mâché, clay, plasticine, glue, sellotape, string, scissors, and so on.

To the experienced teacher all of this is obvious, but even he cannot foresee all the exigencies that are likely to arise once the investigation is under way. The golden rule is not to embark on it empty-handed!

(d) SHARING OUT THE WORK

The next step is to form the pupils into groups. Having been involved in the mapping out of the fields of study, they should have their own views as to which they would like to appropriate. There is, of course, a limit to the extent to which they are free to choose, since it has already been decided how many groups there will be and it is an advantage if these are of roughly equal size. Haloes surround the figures of Drake and Hawkins to which the nameless beggar harassed by the Elizabethan Poor Law cannot aspire, and some topics have a more immediate appeal than others.

Some topics are also more intrinsically difficult than others, and this is reflected in the composition of each field of study, as another glance at the list on pages 61–62 will show. And so it is a matter not only of satisfying an interest, but of matching an ability.

The grouping cannot be settled without reference to the work which immediately preceded it, and the following questions arise: To what extent should a child be allowed to opt for the same aspect of history time and time again? One who has on a previous occasion made a special study of, say, methods of warfare may well want to pursue it. Some teachers believe in giving as much rein as possible to an interest acquired in this way, while others would argue that it is their business to see to it that the range of interests is broadened.

The second question is one of personal relationship, which always plays an important part in any kind of communal activity. If certain members of the class have got on well with one another in the past, is there any objection to their staying together? Or should the groups be re-formed on every occasion, as a matter of principle? All that can be said here is that the answers to these questions must vary with individual circumstances.

The objections to leaving the tasks of finding out and assembling the findings entirely to the pupils can be met to a large degree by the adoption of two alternative methods. Both of these entail that the teacher and class join forces. According to the first, they tackle the era consecutively; according to the second, they tackle it concurrently.

If the first method is followed, the teacher not only provides, as he normally does, an introduction to the era, but goes over it very rapidly by giving an outline of its main features. The children then get down to their work in groups. A number of advantages arise out of this.

Much can be done during the preliminary remarks to redress the balance of popularity between the different fields of study, and as the pupils are no longer in uncharted territory they should find it easier to make up their minds. For the same reason, they may be expected to embark on their assignments with more speed and confidence and require less assistance in carrying them out. Furthermore, the task of drawing together the strands, after the reports have been presented, is no longer quite so formidable. For, having had the ground sketched out for them beforehand, the groups have already some idea of what to expect and there is a greater likelihood of the presentations having more meaning.

This last advantage is missing if ordinary class teaching and group work are carried out not consecutively, but concurrently. Here the children break fresh ground and the element of surprise and novelty is preserved. But the main appeal of the second alternative is that the teacher is in a position to reserve certain aspects of an era for himself, and he will naturally choose those which are either too abstract to lend themselves to a practical representation, or too difficult for his charges to grasp on their own. It is with such considerations in mind that, at the planning stage, an era will be parcelled out into its component fields of study.

Tackling the work from both ends at once also means that the study can be completed in a shorter space of time than if the pupils had been in charge of it all. It can be so arranged that the teacher and groups alternate either within one lesson period, or from lesson to lesson, or from week to week.

Which of these alternative courses of action is followed is a matter of individual preference. As will have been seen, their adoption forestalls many of the difficulties which cannot otherwise be avoided. This applies also to the source material. If there are any aspects of an era about which relevant reading matter cannot be obtained for the pupils' use, the teacher is ready to step in and supply the data himself. If the available information is not adequate, he is there to supplement it, and in cases where it is too detailed, he will be able to extract the salient points and indicate what can be left out.

7

The Era Approach in Action (II): Exploration and Reporting

(*a*) COLLECTING THE INFORMATION

By now each group knows what to do, which is, first of all, to find out all about its chosen field of study and, then, to communicate the results to the rest of the class. The second part is a necessary complement of the first. For, as was previously pointed out, it is vital for each group to know something of the work of the others if the era study is to have any meaning at all.

There are more ways than one in which the information can be obtained. It is, for instance, possible to allocate the various topics within one field to the individual members at the very beginning. If this is done, the considerable specialization which is entailed must be borne in mind. For the purposes of the account which follows, it is assumed that all members of a group explore the same ground initially.

Later on, when it comes to communicating what has been discovered, a variety of techniques can be employed. But for the time being, all groups are engaged in the same task, that of familiarizing themselves with their respective fields of study. The obvious way of going about this is to consult books and to take notes.

In seeking out the necessary information, pupils are in need of guidance, which the teacher can give to a greater or lesser extent. He can either issue duplicated instruction sheets with detailed page references, or go to the opposite extreme of providing only a minimum of clues in the first place and giving no further help unless asked for it. A proper balance must be struck, so that the children are neither spoon fed nor waste time aimlessly turning over pages. The one is as undesirable as the other.

It goes without saying that the younger or less intelligent the children are, or the less experienced at working on their own, the more help they require in learning what to look for. During the time that the class is engaged in reading, writing or making sketches, the teacher can expect to be no less busy, supervising the quest for sources, checking notes, suggesting ways in which the notes can be utilized and making arrangements for the reporting sessions.

(b) RECORDING THE FINDINGS

Once the raw material has been assembled, the next step is to mould it into a presentable shape. The practice which is most widespread is to compile a group book (or folder). Basically, this consists of a series of articles which, together, offer a composite account of the field of study as explored by the group.

The book will, however, contain much more besides straight articles: a map of London in the sixteenth century, for instance, a picture of the Queen, or a drawing of a ducking stool. Illustrations of this kind are an effective means of conveying information, often more economical and striking than the written word.

The corporate effort begins in earnest when the layout of the book is being planned. To begin with, it must be decided what contribution each member is to make, and here the resources of the group can be pooled. It will be found useful for each group to have a leader, to help with co-ordinating the various contributions and supervision in general.

The contributions can be so arranged that the book is divided into different chapters, according to the subject matter for which each member has made himself responsible. They can also be shared out on a purely technical basis, by allocating jobs not according to the contents of the book, but the manner in which it is to be compiled. In the latter case, some pupils will be engaged throughout on writing up the articles, some with illustrating them, and others with paging up and binding.

As far as is practicable, preferences should be taken into consideration. One pupil may offer to take care of Sir Walter Raleigh, because during the initial period of reading he became intrigued with this colourful character, whilst another, with an interest in transport, may be keen to make a drawing of a stage-wagon which made its first appearance in England at about that time. Another, again, may volunteer to do the lettering at which he is the acknowledged expert.

It is important that first drafts be checked and corrected before they are written up, for, apart from making mistakes, children have a disconcerting habit of copying straight from works of reference, and then not necessarily the relevant passages! To issue instructions in the form of questions at the outset, so designed that they cannot be readily answered by copying, is a useful precautionary measure, as is an insistence that references be stated.

It need hardly be stressed that, irrespective of the way in which the book is produced, it should have a cover and title page, include a bibliography, table of contents and index, and the contributions should be signed by the respective authors. If the sheets on which the articles have been written and drawings made are not of uniform size, they can be put into a loose-leaf folder.

When the exploration is undertaken by Juniors, the emphasis will be more on the pictorial presentation of the findings than on written accounts. Pictures can be imaginary drawings or copied from books, traced or cut out. Illustrations often look best if they have been executed on large sheets of paper, in which case their place is not between two covers, but on the walls of the classroom so as to form a frieze.

It would be a mistake to assume that the results of an inquiry can be registered only on paper. Hence it will not come as a surprise if a member of Group I (*Houses and Domestic Life*) attempts to portray the costumes of the age by dressing up dolls, whereas in Group 5 (*Arts and Pastimes*) another member may be busy constructing a replica of the Globe Theatre. There is ample scope for models. Lest it be thought that these are capable only of depicting the social elements in history, attention is drawn to dioramas in which dramatic incidents can be portrayed by toy figures set against a simple scenic background. However, to build any model from scratch requires much time and skill, and what are envisaged here are simple plastic or cut-out models.

Apart from these and similar examples of presenting evidence in concrete terms, there are other, entirely different methods of utilizing the knowledge gained during the period of exploration, as will be seen below.

(c) PRESENTING THE FINDINGS

If the findings have been put down on paper, the books or folders can be passed from group to group, either to be read out aloud or perused quietly. The articles and illustrations may also be used for discussion in class, or form the basis for further written work set by the teacher.

Then there are the various displays. Large-scale drawings and diagrams will in any case be pinned up on the walls, for all to see. The models can be put on show on shelves and tables, though not without brief descriptive labels. In this way an atmosphere can be created in the classroom which will help children to recapture something of the spirit of an age long gone by.

But it must be remembered that, no matter how spectacular the exhibits may be, their presence alone is no guarantee that they will be looked at intelligently and their significance appreciated. For this to happen, the exhibits need to be interpreted, and there is no better way of doing it than to ask the pupils responsible for them to describe them. It is not till a model of the 'Golden Hind' is held up in front of the class by one of the enthusiasts who helped to construct it and the decks and rigging pointed out, that a really lasting impression is made of what an Elizabethan sailing ship was like.

This leads to other, no less effective techniques whereby the groups can report their findings to one another and learn something of the other aspects of the era in question. It is not at all essential for the original notes to be written up or fair-copies of the drawings made; the originals can be used as the raw material for short talks, or 'lecturettes', given by representatives of the various groups.

Many such lecturettes will be illustrated: on the blackboard, for example, by a sketch-map following the course of the Armada, or a genealogical table unravelling Mary Stuart's claim to the English throne, whilst others may be accompanied by pictures shown through the epidiascope. The lecturette-type of approach is particularly useful when the subject matter does not lend itself readily to presentation in concrete form, such as the reasons why Elizabeth I never married. Oral reporting, moreover, does not take up so much time as making up a book and has the further advantage of giving youngsters valuable experience in appearing in front of others and addressing an audience.

Dramatization offers possibilities of a different order, perhaps a mime designed to show a typical day at Court or a series of dramatic episodes from the life of Sir Walter Raleigh. A mock trial of a Roman Catholic priest will convey something about the religious strife of the times, as will the apprehension of a vagrant about changes on the land.

Another way of portraying historical characters in action is to bring in puppets, dressed in authentic costume. Pageants or tableaux, on the other hand, are ideal for re-enacting ceremonials or illustrating aspects of daily life in the days of the Tudors, though they constitute more ambitious projects in which the whole class may well be involved.

The group reporting on *Arts and Pastimes* may be expected to play a piece of music on the recorder, sing a madrigal or perform a country dance. Where there is a lack of musical talent, the aid of a gramophone or tape-recorder can be enlisted. The use of the tape-recorder, in fact, opens up many exciting possibilities.

On the occasion when an era study has been particularly successful, there is every justification for inviting the rest of the school to share in it. This may take the form of a grand exhibition held in the classroom or school hall, or perhaps some of the items are incorporated in the annual concert or play production.

These are but a few examples of how the various findings can be demonstrated and turned to good use. The methods which are adopted depend on the subject matter a particular historical period offers. They depend also on the resources on which the school can draw; on what the children enjoy doing and what they are capable of doing; and, not least, on the person of the teacher, his range of knowledge, his organizing ability and, above all, his enthusiasm.

No two schemes ever turn out alike, especially if a determined effort is made to employ a variety of methods. Some schemes, for example those which involve the construction of models or production of plays, can be very time-consuming. This is why it is an advantage if close co-operation has been established with other departments: with woodwork in the first example and English in the second. Otherwise written accounts and illustrations or, in the case of older pupils, oral reporting will almost certainly form the backbone of the presentations.

Seeing that each group has spent the exploratory phase of an era study on different assignments, the effectiveness of the above-mentioned techniques may well be questioned. Clearly, it is unrealistic to expect every member of the class to obtain a sound grasp of the entire era under review, no matter how carefully the material may be first chosen and subsequently communicated. Without having had the opportunity of sharing in the day-to-day work in which others have been engaged, but merely being confronted with the results of their findings, no pupil is in a position to know as much about their work as he is about his own.

The only hope of achieving this would be to curtail the time allotted to the exploratory phase, in favour of a more thorough exchange of results at the end. The effect would undoubtedly be an overdose of information, not so stodgy perhaps as is normally served up and hence more palatable, but nonetheless indigestible because of the sheer bulk of it. Nothing, in fact, can take the place of direct experience for creating an impression which is deep and lasting.

To attain a mastery in his particular field, to see the significance of it against the general background of the age, and to have, in addition, a fair knowledge and understanding of the contributions made by his fellows—this is as much as can reasonably be expected of a boy or girl at this stage in the proceedings.

Finally, a teacher may wish to test his pupils on their grasp of the aspects of which they made a special study. A good device is to ask each group to come forward in turn, in order to act as a panel or brains trust at which he fires questions. It will not take long before it is revealed whether there has been a genuine penetration into the past, or whether there has been wholesale copying and mechanical assembling of undigested scraps of information. If, on the other hand, the pupils are to be tested on the knowledge acquired about the era as a whole—and not only their respective fields of study—this too can be done by oral questioning or, more systematically, by a written examination.

(d) LINKING THE ERA

Nothing of what has been said so far goes to meet any of the objections arising from the short chronological extent of an era, which means that there is a break between one era and the next with nothing to link them with each other. What can be done to indicate their place in time and maintain the thread of continuity? There are several devices, one of which is the time chart.

Normally, the aid of a chart is invoked when a large amount of detailed information has been assembled and the items extend over a large tract of time. It then acts as an orderly framework in which the items can be tabulated and the connection between them shown. But when, as in this case, the number of years covered is relatively small, the time chart fulfils a different purpose. It shows that an era is part of the process of historical evolution and pinpoints its exact location in that process. At the same time, it cannot fail to serve as a reminder of how much has been deliberately omitted.

What about the gaps that remain? If they are filled in, it is important that two conditions are observed: one is that only the most salient dates and facts are entered, and the other that the pupils are not required to learn by heart what, since it has merely been copied down, has no meaning to them. The only justification for making these additional entries is that they can be used as points of reference for future occasions, and provide signposts for independent reading to which a good teacher knows how to direct his pupils.

In this, as in any other approach to the teaching of history, the effectiveness of time charts must, however, not be overrated. The number of hours and meticulous care lavished on them is often quite out of proportion to the results achieved, and a knowledge of consecutive data must not be confused with an understanding of a time sequence. The former can be mechanically acquired; the latter takes years to mature.

What will surely help to develop in the minds of children a feeling for time and sense of perspective, is a scheme in which the eras succeed one another in chronological order. It may be objected that this will restore one of the principal evils of the traditional outline approach, its strict adherence to chronology which was condemned on the grounds that it paid no regard to the mental and emotional development of young people. The objection can be met if the subject matter *within* an era is always carefully graded. Another suggestion is to study the same eras more than once during the school course, each time at a more advanced level, according to the concentric principle.

Perhaps the most satisfactory way of all of doing justice to the element of continuity in history is to invest each era with points of contact, or 'feelers', so that it no longer stands in a timeless vacuum. Both teacher and pupils can do much towards this end: the teacher, by devoting more time than he usually does to introducing a new era and using this introduction in order to place it in its historical setting and establish vital links with the inquiry which has just been completed; the pupils, by treating their fields of study in a more flexible manner, if at liberty to go back in time to some appropriate starting point. To take the Elizabethan Age as an illustration again, no one need feel mesmerized by the date 1558, and the group grappling with the religious settlement of Elizabeth has to know something of the policy of her predecessor.

Similarly, there will be freedom to look ahead so that, where appropriate, certain topics can be followed beyond what would ordinarily be the chronological dead-line. This will make it possible to bring the topics to a point where they can be conveniently rounded off. Some of these points will act as bridge-heads with which contact can be established later on (for example, first American colonies).

There is, however, a limit to which one may go if all this is not to become a pale imitation of teaching by outlines.

The teacher must never allow himself to become obsessed with the process of 'filling the gaps', which can be done only by summaries, nor the pupils spend as much time outside the era as they do inside. If this were to happen, the time allocated for the study of the era itself would be so curtailed as to make a thorough investigation of it an impossibility. And without attention to detail, the object of the approach is defeated.

Nor is the answer to attempt to bridge the interval between two eras by means of formal homework. Where homework is the rule, it should, as in any other subject, be integrated with the work done in class. To encourage children to go on reading in their own time is a different matter. Once they have been inspired, they will do so in any case.

Inevitably, much factual information will have been missed out. The short period of history must remain the basic unit, but it will have to be treated in a flexible way, so that it is not cut off from the main stream of historical events. What it boils down to, in effect, is that the eras are attached to a broad chronological framework.

But is this all? Is not the ultimate purpose of subjecting a child to the experience of 'getting under the skin' of an age other than his own and furnishing him with the tools wherewith to realize this experience, that he should develop a critical awareness of the age in which he lives? It is only when he applies the same awareness to the present as he has been trained to apply to the past and appreciates the essential resemblances and differences between them, that he can fully understand the present.

When the results of the explorations are reported, the teacher must do more, therefore, than act the part of master-of-ceremonies. He must do more even than blend the various contributions into an intelligible whole, so that a complete image of an era emerges. His is also the responsibility to ensure that comparisons are established between conditions as they were and conditions as they are and the necessary inferences drawn. This further step is imperative and shows the teacher at his most indispensable.

There will be many occasions when children will need little or no prompting to form their own conclusions from a contrast when they come across it, between for instance the sanitary arrangements of a Tudor hovel and a modern Council house. At other times, a good deal of explanation is necessary before it is appreciated what, say, the persecutions of religious minorities in the sixteenth century have in common with the racial persecutions of the twentieth century.

What we must not do is to make every history lesson an object lesson, to drag in material for the sole purpose of propounding a contemporary problem or to contrive every situation so as to be able to extract a moral from it. History is no more (nor less) a vocational subject than any other subject in the school curriculum, and the times when it can be left to 'tell its own story' occur more often than is sometimes admitted.

8

Conclusion

When framing the syllabus, it is helpful to look upon history as a three-dimensional subject which requires treatment in length, breadth and depth. That is to say, to show what happened at any given place and time is not enough. It is also necessary to find out what led up to it and what followed; to know what it owed, or contributed, to contemporaneous events; and to present the evidence in full, without which there can be no real understanding. This is the ideal after which the teacher of history must strive. How can it be attained?

The traditional answer, and in theory the correct answer, is to pay each dimension the same amount of attention. But what happens when this is put into practice, our discussion of the traditional syllabus showed: by trying to do justice to them all, justice is done to none, and the dimension that usually suffers most is depth. The scaffolding is there, but nothing inside it.

The reformer is determined not to make the same mistake. He is right in his diagnosis that depth is of cardinal importance, but wrong in adding to it either length *or* breadth. A typical example of the former error is the 'line of development' and of the latter, of course, the 'era'. Inevitably, the structure is lop-sided.

One way of ensuring that none of the three dimensions is lost sight of is to place them in order of priority. Depth should always come first, and whether length is followed by breadth, or breadth by length, will lay down the general lines along which the syllabus is to be constructed. In the case of the *modified* era approach, the longitudinal direction is placed last, but the essential thing is that it has not been left out.

At the same time as the syllabus is constructed, consideration has to be given to the means by which it is best implemented. For just as the most up-to-date techniques and aids to teaching are wasted on subject matter which is basically unsound, the past can never be brought to life if the methods of presentation are poor. From the very beginning matter and method must be geared to each other, and the one must not dominate the other. The classic example of the last being allowed to happen is provided by the old-fashioned type of history teaching, in which the pupils are passive recipients.

Here, too, the reformer diagnoses the situation correctly, but he overestimates the capabilities of children to find out for themselves and to utilize their findings to the best advantage. It seems reasonable therefore, to suggest a compromise, and what the *modified* era approach attempts to do is to harness the resources of the pupils and the teacher so that they become partners in a joint venture.

It should not be inferred from the previous account that the success of the approach is contingent on the class operating in groups. Many teachers prefer individual assignments, and, indeed, within groups the actual work is done by individuals. What both methods have in common is that the pupils are working at their tasks by themselves, under guidance.

What remains of the original era approach? Although it has been severely handled, it has not lost its essential character. It still differs from the conventional outline presentation in two significant respects. The material has been drastically reduced according to a reasoned principle, and this material is treated in such a way that the pupils play a full part. If, in addition, the comparative element is not neglected, it is very much in line with modern thinking which recognizes the need for relating the past to the present.

One can then say without reservation that the modified version is not only an acceptable alternative to the conventional approach, but an improvement on it. Whether it is also superior to other departures from tradition is another matter. It stands to reason that they, too, would similarly gain from being revised and adapted.

There is yet another way of doing justice to the three dimensions which has not yet been mentioned. That is to maintain a clear distinction between them and to concentrate sometimes on the one and sometimes on the other. It means, for example, engaging for a while on a piece of local history, next pursuing a significant trend over a period of years, and then perhaps lingering over a particular scene. Such a procedure does not conflict with the criterion laid down earlier. For, although extracting special aspects from the common matter of history involves the total exclusion of at least one of the three dimensions at any one time, the exclusion is only temporary.

The fact has to be faced that, given the conditions under which he operates, the history teacher cannot avoid making concessions. No matter what course of action he may embark on, none will give him all he asks. He has no option but to select, and to select means to sacrifice. What he must be quite clear about in his mind is the direction in which the sacrifice lies, and the question he has to ask himself in each case is to what extent a loss in one direction is outweighed by a gain in another.

The decision is largely individual in view of the wide divergence of opinion regarding the aims of the subject, ranging from the purely utilitarian to the purely cultural. And where there is no agreement on the fundamental question of aims, agreement cannot be expected on the question of contents. Hence any attempt to establish an agreed history syllabus is doomed from the start.

Many schemes have been drawn up. The scheme a teacher

adopts in his school is not necessarily the one which looks most attractive on paper, but one which in his particular circumstances works out most satisfactorily in practice. It will then be subject to continual change in the light of experience. There is no better way of arriving at a final assessment than by giving different schemes a trial.

In that respect those who teach history in this country are in a more fortunate position than their colleagues abroad, most of whom have their syllabuses prescribed for them by some external authority. They also have an advantage over their colleagues at home in charge of other subjects. For, as has already been pointed out, as far as sheer knowledge is concerned, there is no essential groundwork which has to be mastered first, nor need the requirements of public examinations be a disturbing factor. There is, therefore, freedom and ample scope for experiment.

In attempting to arrive at an assessment of any particular approach, it is advisable not to make extravagant claims on behalf of the subject as a whole. Much of what it is hoped the past will convey cannot be taught by direct means, and it may not make itself felt until adulthood is reached. In any case, it can never be directly assessed.

The real test lies not so much in the amount of factual knowledge a child gains from the study of history at school. The important thing is whether the knowledge gained in a relatively limited field is such that it has equipped him to deduce general principles on which to base judgment, and developed an attitude of wanting to increase and utilize the knowledge for the rest of his life.

APPENDIX 1

A Suggested Syllabus

The syllabus below has been designed for use in secondary schools. It must be viewed against the background of what was said on pages 3–12 from which the uniqueness of every history syllabus emerged, and pages 59–61 in which attention was drawn to the many variable speculiar to the era approach.

The disadvantage of producing such a scheme is that, invariably, it satisfies none but the author. The advantage is that it helps to pinpoint some of the problems, for example those of deciding at which strategic point in time to pitch an era, and how to define its breadth and length.

The syllabus comprises 24 eras, which means that in a four-year course two eras are allocated to each term. The contents of any of them can be made easier, or more difficult, as the occasion demands. A teacher with five years at his disposal is in a position to explore the same number more fully, or to add to the total number. However, what matters is not how many eras there are but what they are about, and it is to be hoped that those to whom this approach appeals will modify the syllabus or, better still, produce one of their own.

(1) *The Stone Age*

The three great periods of prehistory are the Palaeolithic Age, Neolithic Age and Bronze Age. Although the first two extend over several hundred thousand years, they may be treated as an entity, the theme being man's first appearance on earth, how he had to fend for himself and what progress he made even before he discovered the use of metal.

The Bronze Age is included in the next era.

(2) *Egypt under the Pharaohs*

There is no point in taking separately and in chronological sequence the early civilizations of the Egyptians, Babylonians, Assyrians, Hebrews, Indians and Chinese.

Egypt is a representative, and probably the most spectacular, example. The period from *c.* 1500 to 1200 B.C. is recommended because during the eighteenth and nineteenth dynasties the kingdom reached its zenith; and since it stretched as far as the Euphrates, links can readily be established with the history of Mesopotamia.

(3) *Fifth Century Athens*

Ideally, one would want to cover the whole of Ancient Greece, from the early myths to Alexander the Great. But if only one era is possible, the obvious choice is the fifth century, during which Athens, victorious against the Persians and humbled by the Spartans, became the cultural capital.

(4) *Rome and Carthage*

To do justice to the history of Rome presents a formidable task, in view of the great number of years (about 1100) and territorial expanse involved. However, without going into the internal dissensions and military campaigns in detail, most of the salient features can be crowded into two eras (one republican, the other imperial). The first may be set in the third century B.C., which is not too late to paint a picture of a vigorous and upcoming nation against the background of a thrilling story.

(5) *Roman Britain*

This era serves as an introduction to British history, with a backward glance at prehistoric times. Because of the many remains dating from the Iron Age and period of Roman occupation, it can often be treated from a local angle.

If, at the same time, Britain is placed in the wider context of the Empire, an opportunity is afforded of comparing

Rome at its height (A.D. 98–180) with the earlier pioneering days. The Emperor Hadrian is the obvious link.

(6) *The Time of King Alfred*

The second half of the ninth century may be used to summarize the changes which had come over the British Isles since the departure of the Romans, as a result of the Anglo-Saxon and Danish invasions and the spread of Christianity.

(7) *The Coming of the Normans*

The emphasis will be on the immediate effects of the Norman invasion, rather than the steps which led up to it, which can be quickly dealt with. Domesday Book provides much information of local interest, as do castles, abbeys or parish churches. All this will give a good picture of early medieval society in general.

(8) *The Near and Far East*

The Third Crusade, the conquests of Genghis Khan and the visit of Marco Polo to the court of Kublai Khan offer much interesting material, besides serving as an antidote to undue insularity.

(Nearer home, because of the underlying unity of medieval Christendom, the story of any of the following people or occasions can be broadened in such a way that it yields much of the essence of the times as a whole: Frederick Barbarossa, Eleanor of Aquitaine, Thomas Becket, St. Francis of Assisi, Magna Carta, Simon de Montfort, Conquest of Wales, Robert Bruce, Swiss Everlasting League.)

(9) *The World of Chaucer*

This era represents the later Middle Ages and can be based on the characters which figure in the Prologue to Chaucer's *Canterbury Tales*, such as the

> Knight, Yeoman, Squire (Chivalry, Armour, Hundred Years' War)
> Monk, Friar, Parson (The Church)

> Reeve, Miller, Ploughman (The Manor, Peasants' Revolt)
>
> Wife of Bath, Merchant, Haberdasher etc. (Towns, Trade)

(10) *The Renaissance Era*

The fifteenth century may be by-passed without great loss, but not the political, religious, cultural and economic ferment of the turn of the century, as it affected Europe and the New World. Much of it is highly complex, but one way of making it intelligible is to make the approach through the leading personalities, for example

> Henry VIII, Wolsey, Charles V (Governments and nations)
>
> Luther, Calvin, Thomas Cromwell (Reformation)
>
> Gutenberg, Leonardo da Vinci, Copernicus (Renaissance)
>
> Columbus, Magellan, Pizarro (Geographical discoveries)

(11) *The Days of Queen Elizabeth I*

This era lends itself particularly well to the cross-sectional kind of treatment. How it can be tackled has been described in detail in Chapters 6 and 7.

(12) *The Restoration Period*

The seventeenth century merits one era. The difficulty is to do justice to the struggle between King and Parliament through all the phases:

> (1) Causes of the conflict
> (2) Course of the Civil War
> (3) The interregnum
> (4) The Restoration
> (5) The Revolution Settlement

The advantage of picking one of the middle phases is that it can always be extended in either direction. The preference here is for (4) since it seems logical to regard results as more important than origins. Besides, it is rich in social material and saw the beginning of the struggle with France and further overseas expansion.

(13) *The Age of Revolutions (I): Britain*

Here we have an example of a more ambitious type of study, which has been divided into three eras and on which, therefore, a term and a half's work is spent. As the title suggests, there is a common theme: CHANGE.

We begin with changes in Britain, by looking at society as it existed in the middle of the eighteenth century and examining the impact on it of advances in industry, agriculture and transport, of Methodism, etc.

(14) *The Age of Revolutions (II): Europe*

We need only concentrate on the years from 1789 to 1815, to find that they are packed with events of momentous importance. One suggestion is to cover them in outline first and then to allocate 'special periods' to groups of pupils, as follows: 1789–1795; 1795–1802; 1802–1807; 1807–1812; 1812–1815.

Even so, there must be ruthless selection, particularly in the military and diplomatic sphere, so that the changes which resulted from the upheavals emerge clearly at the end.

(15) *The Age of Revolutions (III): Overseas*

The trilogy is completed with a survey of the major changes in the rest of the world during this period. They include events in India and Canada as a result of the Seven Years' War; the voyages of Captain Cook; the achieving of American Independence; the capture of Cape Town; and the liberation of South America.

(16) *Mid-Victorian Times*

The scene shifts to the middle of the nineteenth century where, at home, the industrial growth and its social effects are bound to loom large. The Great Exhibition of 1851 makes

YEAR I

The Stone Age
Egypt under the Pharaohs

Fifth Century Athens

Rome and Carthage

Roman Britain

B.C. 900 800 700 600 500 400 300 200 100 | 100 200 300 400 500

A.D.		Year 2	Year 3	Year 4
600				
700				
800				
900	The Time of King Alfred			
1000				
1100		The Coming of the Normans		
1200		The Near and Far East		
1300				
1400		The World of Chaucer		
1500		The Renaissance Era / The Days of Queen Elizabeth I		
1600		The Restoration Period		
1700				
1800		The Age of Revolutions: (I) Britain (II) Europe (III) Overseas	Mid-Victorian Times / America during the Civil War	
1900			The British Empire at its Height	The Edwardian Scene / The Struggle for Power / The 'Thirties
A.D.			The Second World War / The Nuclear Age	Britain in the Nuclear Age

16

a good focal point. At the same time, it is desirable to look beyond the domestic scene, to the struggle of nationalism and liberalism in Europe, using perhaps only Germany as an example.

The mid-century also saw some remarkable publications which provide an entirely different (but very difficult) approach to the times, for example

> 1847: Marx *Communist Manifesto* (Class Struggle)
> 1849: Ruskin *The Seven Lamps of Architecture* (Gothic Revival)
> 1859: Darwin *Origin of Species* (Theory of Evolution)
> 1859: Tennyson *Idylls of the King* (Patriotism)
> 1859: Mill *On Liberty* (Social Control)
> 1864: Newman *Apologia pro vita sua* (Catholic Revival)

(17) *America during the Civil War*

In the present scheme this is the only era which is devoted entirely to the United States of America, as exemplified by the most crucial landmark in their historical evolution.

(18) *The British Empire at its Height*

This is the only study made exclusively of the British overseas territories, as they were in *c.* 1900 when expansion was beginning to be superseded by self-determination. A comparison with the position today will, of course, be invited.

(If desired, the entire history of the British Empire and Commonwealth could be broken up into separate eras, so that either the whole territorial extent is covered at certain chronological intervals, or only parts. For India alone, 1757, 1857, and 1947 would be appropriate landmarks.)

(19) *The Edwardian Scene*

The whole of the last year of the four-year course is spent on the present century. Everything is so inter-connected that any divisions are artificial. But because there is so much that should be made known, there is still virtue in concentration.

As far as Britain is concerned, the downfall of the Conservatives in 1905 marks a turning point politically. But there are many other indications of the approach of a new epoch, as exemplified by wireless telegraphy, suffragettes, aeroplanes, the *Daily Mirror* and the *Dreadnought*.

(20) *The Struggle for Power*

A comparison of the world as it was in 1914 with that of 1918, a minimum of time being spent on the war itself.

This is the first serious attempt at a world perspective. It can be built up either by investigating separately such aspects as international relations, political systems, industrial conditions and cultural achievements; or by covering all of these continent by continent.

(21) *The 'Thirties*

The object here is to summarize the pre-war years at home and abroad, that is the general situation before the Second World War as well as the circumstances which led up to the war.

The difficulty of selection may be eased a little by giving the era a theme (though generalizations are always dangerous): FAILURE. Failure to solve the economic crisis and failure to save the League of Nations.

(22) *The Second World War*

Unlike any other war, this war affected every facet of life, so that a strong case can be made out for subjecting it to a close scrutiny.

(23) *The Nuclear Age*

Throughout the course, the 'Then and Now' technique of comparison will have been followed. But it is fitting that the most recent trends and events should receive ample treatment in their own right. This is attempted by the last two eras.

The first is a survey of the major issues facing the world today, prefaced by the most important international developments since 1945.

(24) *Britain in the Nuclear Age*

Finally, the survey is narrowed down to a more particular study of the mother country, employing Anthony Sampson's method of inquiry in his *Anatomy of Britain* (Hodder and Stoughton, 1962), but not confining it to institutions.

APPENDIX 2

A List of Reference Books

The most comprehensive and up-to-date surveys of available books and other source material are to be found in the *Handbook for History Teachers* ed. W. H. BURSTON and C. W. GREEN (Methuen, 1962, 25/-) and the *Guide to Illustrative Material for Use in Teaching History* comp. G. A. WILLIAMS (The Historical Association, 1962, 8/6).

The bibliography below is confined to what are commonly called reference, information or background books, which together constitute a series. Class textbooks, biographical series and encyclopaedias are not included. Lack of space does not permit listing each individual volume in a series (many of them are still expanding), and any classification would be misleading without going into considerable detail.

All the series contain books which are suitable for children engaged in finding out for themselves historical information of a specific nature. The best way of ascertaining which are appropriate is to consult the above *Handbook* and *Guide*, obtain catalogues from the publishers whose names and addresses are given here in alphabetical order and, finally, send for inspection copies. The prices which are stated here are accurate at the time of going to press.

Picture Source Books for Social History ed. MOLLY HARRISON *et al.*
12/6 to 15/- each
George Allen & Unwin Ltd., 40 Museum St. London, W.C.1

Understanding the Modern World
4/6 each   Allen & Unwin

The St. George's Library
12/6 each
Edward Arnold Ltd., 41 Maddox Street, London, W.1

The Rockliff New Project Histories
Background booklets 2/-, practical books 6/6 to 8/6 each
Barrie & Rockliff, 2 Clement's Inn, Strand, London, W.C.2

Junior Heritage Books
8/6 each
B. T. Batsford Ltd., 4 Fitzhardinge Street, London, W.1

A History of Everyday Things in England M. AND C. H. B. QUENNELL
21/- each   Batsford

Everyday Life and Everyday Things
21/- each   Batsford

English Life Series ed. PETER QUENNELL
21/- each   Batsford

Black's Junior Reference Books ed. R. J. UNSTEAD
8/6 to 10/6 each
A. & C. Black, 4–6 Soho Square, London, W.1

Social Life in England JOHN FINNEMORE
7/6 to 8/6 each   Black

They Saw It Happen
17/6 to 30/- each
Basil Blackwell & Mott Ltd., 49 Broad Street, Oxford
How They Lived
35/- each   Blackwell

Blackwell's Pocket Histories
9/6 each   Blackwell

The Study Books ed. RAY MITCHELL
9/6 each
The Bodley Head Ltd., 10 Earlham Street, London, W.C.2

World Culture Series
12/6 to 16/- each
Brockhampton Press Ltd., Market Place, Leicester

Journeys Through Our Early History ed. COLIN CLAIR
6/- each
Bruce & Gawthorn Ltd., 21–23 Market St., Watford, Herts.

What Was Their Life? ed. RAYMOND FAWCETT
6/– each   Bruce & Gawthorn

Man and His Conquests
15/– each
Burke Publishing Co. Ltd., 14 John Street, London, W.C.1

Jackdaws ed. JOHN LANGDON-DAVIES
9/6 each wallet
Jonathan Cape Ltd., 30 Bedford Square, London, W.C.1

Cassell Caravel Books
21/– each
Cassell & Co. Ltd., 35 Red Lion Square, London, W.C.1

Dawn of History RICHARD CARRINGTON
3/6 each
Chatto & Windus Ltd., 40–42 William IV St., London, W.C.2

The Story of . . . AGNES ALLEN
12/6 to 18/– each
Faber & Faber Ltd., 24 Russell Square, London, W.C.1

History Bookshelves ed. CATHERINE B. FIRTH
Sets of six booklets, 6/– to 7/– each set
Ginn & Co. Ltd., 18 Bedford Row, London, W.C.1

Museum Bookshelves ed. CATHERINE B. FIRTH
Sets of six booklets, 7/6 to 8/6 each set   Ginn

Look Books
4/9 each
Hamish Hamilton, 90 Great Russell Street, London, W.C.1

This Wonderful World
3/6 each
George G. Harrap & Co. Ltd., 182 High Holborn, London, W.C.1

Great Civilizations C. A. BURLAND
6/– each
Hulton Educational Publications Ltd., 55–59 Saffron Hill, London, E.C.1

Children in History MOLLY HARRISON
5/6 each   Hulton

Portraits and Documents gen. ed. J. S. MILLWARD
7/6 to 9/6 each
Hutchinson Educational Ltd., 178–202 Great Portland Street,
London, W.1

Then and There ed. M. E. REEVES
3/6 to 5/- each
Longmans, Green & Co. Ltd., 48 Grosvenor St., London, W.1

Man's Heritage ed. E. H. DANCE
4/6 each   Longmans

Evidence in Pictures ISLAY DONCASTER
8/- each   Longmans

The Wonderful World (Rathbone Books)
21/- each
Macdonald & Co. Ltd., 2 Portman Street, London, W.1

History Picture Books ed. E. J. S. LAY
3/6 each
Macmillan & Co. Ltd., St. Martin's Street, London, W.C.2

Methuen's Outlines ed. PATRICK THORNHILL
10/6 to 15/- each
Methuen & Co. Ltd., 11 New Fetter Lane, London, E.C.4

Exploring the Past ed. E. ROYSTON PIKE
10/6 each
Frederick Muller Ltd., 110 Fleet Street, London, E.C.4

True Books ed. VERNON KNOWLES
9/6 each   Muller

The Changing Shape of Things
15/- each
John Murray, 50 Albemarle Street, London, W.1

Quest Library
5/- each
Oliver & Boyd Ltd., Tweeddale Court, Edinburgh 1

The Signpost Library
7/6 to 8/6 each   Oliver & Boyd

How They Were Built J. STEWART MURPHY
9/6 to 10/6 each
Oxford University Press, Amen House, Warwick Square, London, E.C.4

People of the Past ed. PHILIPPA PEARCE
2/– each   Oxford University Press

A New Look at World History M. NEURATH and J. A. LAUWERYS
7/6 each
Max Parrish & Co. Ltd., 55 Queen Anne Street, London, W.1

English History in Pictures THE HISTORICAL ASSOCIATION
8/6 each
George Philip & Son Ltd., Victoria Road, London, N.W.10

How Series ed. PHEBE SNOW
10/6 to 12/6 each
Routledge & Kegan Paul Ltd., Broadway House, 68–74 Carter Lane, London, E.C.4

Visual History of Modern Britain ed. JACK SIMMONS
30/– each
Studio Vista Ltd., Blue Star House, Highgate Hill, London, N.19

The Discovery Reference Books ed. ALYS L. GREGORY
7/6 each
University of London Press Ltd., Little Paul's House, Warwick Square, London, E.C.4

First Books
10/6 each
Edmund Ward, 194–200 Bishopsgate, London, E.C.2

How to Explore (Information Books)
9/6 to 10/6 each
Ward Lock Educational Co. Ltd., 116 Baker Street, London, W.1

How Things Developed (Information Books)
9/6 to 10/6 each   Ward Lock

The Young Historian ed. PATRICK MOORE
12/6 each
Weidenfield & Nicolson (Educational) Ltd., 20 New Bond Street, London, W.1

The Wheaton Junior Reference Books
10/6 to 12/6 each
A. Wheaton & Co. Ltd., Fore Street, Exeter

Index

INDEX

INDEX

INDEX